Joseph England is a Barrister at 3 Paper Buildings and a specialist Employment practitioner. His busy practice has ensured he has in-depth experience of a wide variety of areas and types of claim, including significant expertise in whistleblowing cases both within and outside of the NHS. Of note, he acted as junior for the successful Claimant who was awarded £1.22mil in *Mattu v University Hospitals Coventry & Warwickshire NHS Trust* (ET, 1302226/11, 1303494/12) and in the successful appeal in *McTigue v University Hospital Bristol NHS Foundation Trust* ([2016] IRLR 742), which considered the scope of protection for whistleblowers, leading to a wider definition of those who could claim protection. He has also acted for various respondents in whistleblowing cases, including NHS Trusts and Health Boards, Education Institutions and a wide variety of businesses. Further details and examples of cases can be found on his chambers' website.

His success and evident abilities have led clients to trust Joseph with very complex cases. Joseph's practice benefits from representing and advising both sides of employment disputes and he has been instructed in cases at the Court of Appeal, EAT and at a wide range of final and preliminary hearings in tribunal and court. He regularly delivers training covering areas from nuanced and niche points of law to basics of the Tribunal procedure and mock tribunals. He has been published in the ELA Briefing, on Westlaw and provides updates through Chambers and on Twitter @JEnglandCounsel.

NHS Whistleblowing and the Law

NHS Whistleblowing and the Law

Joseph England

LLB (Hons), BA (Hons), PG Dip (Outstanding),
GDL GDip (Commendation)
Barrister, 3 Paper Buildings, Temple

Law Brief Publishing

Published 2019 by Law Brief Publishing, an imprint of Law Brief Publishing Ltd
30 The Parks
Minehead
Somerset
TA24 8BT

www.lawbriefpublishing.com

Paperback: 978-1-912687-35-0

FOREWORD

Whistleblowing matters. It matters in the all sectors of the UK, but as recent experience has shown and this book demonstrates, it matters even more in the NHS.

All organisations, public or private, face the risk that something will go badly wrong and ought to welcome the opportunity to address this as early as possible. Whenever such a situation arises, the first people to know will usually be those who work in the organisation. Knowing about a problem means it can be fixed, a patient safety risk sorted, a disaster averted and a reputation salvaged. But all too often when public inquiries are set up to look into what went wrong, they find that those on the front line knew there was an issue but were too scared to say anything, had been ignored or, worse, were victimised when they tried to speak up.

This book is a timely reminder of why whistleblowers and whistleblowing rights are important in the NHS. As a charity that has worked for over 25 years to gain and strengthen legal rights for those who speak up in the workplace, we know only too well how difficult a whistleblower's journey can be.

The blame culture so prevalent in the NHS has also been the subject of numerous policy initiatives. Issues of openness, transparency and candour were key in the report of the Mid Staffordshire NHS Foundation Trust Public Inquiry (the Francis Report). The duty of candour and the reforms brought in by Sir Robert Francis have resulted in some much-needed change, but these reforms are still bedding in and our experience from those working on the front line is that there is still a long way to go. Piecemeal reform has seen the legal landscape become ever more com-plicated. When the legal protection for whistleblowers was first envisaged, the employment tribunal system was a place where litigants in person could fend for themselves. We are not so sure that this is still the case and so any help available to individuals and those who support them is welcome. We know from our clients the incredible value of timely legal advice, but that too few are aware of the help available, or only know about it when it is too late.

We hope that this book will make the litigants journey an easier one and we will continue our work to try and ensure that fewer individuals end up facing a legal battle in the first place.

Francesca West
Chief Executive
Protect

PREFACE

Whistleblowing – when a person raises a concern about something that is not right – has received increased attention in recent years as a result of several high profile cases and incidents across a wide range of sectors. Within the NHS, the nature of the work, the reality of contemporary funding strains and the dedication of the staff all make for an environment in which whistleblowing is both very important and relatively common. This importance was recognised by the Freedom to Speak Up Review, which opens, "this review was set up in response to continuing disquiet about the way NHS organisations deal with concerns raised by NHS staff and the treatment of those who have spoken up" (page 8, para. 1). Whistleblowing is not meant to be a dirty word and it has never been the intention of the law in this area to convert whistleblowers into either troublemakers or martyrs, as they are sometimes cast. Workers may well make protected disclosures, and thereby become whistleblowers, more frequently than they realise and without subsequent incident. A nurse filling out a Datix entry/clinical incident form as a matter of good practice and to maintain an accurate record is likely to have 'blown the whistle' by technically making a protected disclosure, and such routine reporting of safety concerns occurs of course daily throughout the NHS.

This book will provide a comprehensive and practical guide to the law relating to whistleblowing, focusing on the NHS. The main legislation that will be considered will be the Public Interest Disclosure Act 1998 ("PIDA 1998"), as incorporated into the Employment Rights Act 1996 ("ERA 1996"). This legislation is the main protection for whistleblowers, designed to provide a right not to suffer detriment or dismissal as a result of making a protected disclosure and providing rights to bring legal claims if the contrary occurs. This book will explain the law, providing an explanation and citation of case law as appropriate. Analysis will be useful for both sides of any dispute, whether worker or employer, and although points specific to the NHS will be highlighted where relevant, the legal position is rarely unique to the NHS and this book therefore can be utilised by anyone seeking to understand the law of whistleblowing.

The legislation was significantly amended in June 2013 by the Enterprise and Regulatory Reform Act 2013 ("ERRA 2013"), such as by the insertion of the public interest test. Any claim based on a protected disclosure made after that date will proceed under the new law (s.24(6) ERRA 2013) and therefore in keeping with this book's focus on practicality, this book will focus on the position under the post-2013 law. Whilst some long-running or historic cases will be based on the previous position, this is likely to be a very small number and therefore largely omitted, although this book will explain the previous position where this provides an insight into the reasoning behind the current legal position.

My knowledge of whistleblowing cases is based on extensive and broad experience. As a barrister, I have conducted various whistleblowing cases involving workers both within and outside of the NHS. I acted as junior for the successful Claimant who was awarded £1.22 million in *Mattu v University Hospitals Coventry & Warwickshire NHS Trust* (ET, 1302226/11, 1303494/12) and in the successful appeal in *McTigue v University Hospital Bristol NHS Foundation Trust* ([2016] IRLR 742), which considered the scope of protection for whistleblowers, leading to a wider definition of those who could claim protection. In addition, I have acted for various respondents, including NHS Trusts and Health Boards, Education Institutions and a wide variety of businesses.

I would like to take this opportunity to thank my clerks and colleagues at 3 Paper Buildings who have helped my career develop in this field, particularly Russell Porter, Matthew Scanlan and Patrick Robson, as well as my family and partner Caroline for their ubiquitous support.

This book presents the law as understood at 16th March 2019. The content cannot be relied upon for, nor is it intended to provide, legal advice and in an individual case specific advice should of course be obtained. No liability is accepted for any reliance on the contents of this book.

Joseph England
March 2019

CONTENTS

CHAPTER ONE
POINTS OF PROCEDURE

This chapter is designed to assist the practitioner or litigant in some of the practical elements of pursuing or defending a whistleblower claim. It will focus on the mechanics of a tribunal claim, outlining some tips learned from experience and pitfalls to be avoided. Issues and claims outside of a tribunal will be briefly covered.

<u>Types of Claim</u>

Although this book will concentrate on claims within an employment tribunal, a person who believes they have made a protected disclosure and therefore believes they are a whistleblower has various potential claims or hearings in which they may be involved. A non-exhaustive list includes:

(a) An internal resolution, whether through their employer's whistleblowing or grievance procedure, or both. In early 2016, NHS Improvement and NHS England produced 'Freedom to Speak Up: raising concerns (whistleblowing) policy for the NHS', aimed at being a national standardisation of the way disclosures of concern should be treated. This is addressed in more detail below.

(b) A claim in an employment tribunal that as a result of making a protected disclosure, the individual has suffered a detriment or been dismissed. These claims are the focus of this book.

(c) An application for interim relief, pursuant to s.128 ERA 1996. This is a remedy claimed as part of a claim that dismissal was because of a protected disclosure and if successful, will effectively mean that the employment contract will continue, whether by reinstatement or continuation of pay. Such a claim must be made within 7 days of the effective date of termination and the high threshold a Claimant must meet and further points of procedure are outlined in more detailed in the Remedy chapter.

(d) An application for an injunction, i.e. to prevent something from happening or force a person or organisation to do something. Examples include seeking an injunction to prevent an employer from enacting a decision to dismiss or other detriment that they say has occurred because of a disclosure, or seeking the release of information to allow a person to publish or otherwise use the information. Equally, an employer could seek an injunction, for example to prevent a person from passing information on to an organisation such as the media or to prevent an organisation from publishing confidential information. Such a claim is likely to be issued in the High Court or County Court, depending on what is sought, rather than an employment tribunal, which has very different powers. Accordingly, the governing rules will be those of the Civil Procedure Rules rather than those of the Employment Tribunal and CPR 25 in particular should be consulted. The governing principles from the first stage of interim injunction remain those from *American Cyanamid v Ethicon Ltd* [1975] AC 396 and for examples within the NHS see *Ardron v Sussex Partnership NHS Foundation Trust* [2018] EWHC 3157 (QB, application for an injunction to restrain proceedings for gross misconduct) and *Mattu v University Hospitals of Coventry and Warwickshire NHS Trust* [2012] EWCA Civ 641 (application for a declaration that the dismissal of a consultant was ineffective and for injunctive relief).

(e) An application for judicial review. For an example of an application by a nurse arising out of a decision to hold a meeting of the Professional Conduct Committee, see *Tehrani v United Kingdom Central Council for Nursing, Midwifery and Health Visiting* [2001] IRLR 208.

(f) An application involving s.43J ERA 1996, which states, "any provision in an agreement to which this section applies is void in so far as it purports to preclude the worker from making a protected disclosure". This section is likely to be most relevant to compromise agreements and practitioners will have noted intense focus on non-disclosure agreements recently, put under the spotlight by the events leading up to and around the '#metoo' movement and the scrutiny of various settlement agreements that it is said have covered up wrongdoings, discussed more in the final section alongside the relevance of the national NHS Whistleblowing Guardian. These issues have also arisen in the context of the NHS after media coverage of various whistleblower or alleged whistle-blower cases, such as Gary Walker in 2013 who, it is reported, was dismissed from his position as Lincolnshire Trusts Hospitals Chief Executive after raising concerns about capacity for the non-emergency waiting list.

(g) Other interim applications as part of any of the above. These could include an application for a declaration (see *Mattu*, above) or an application for specific disclosure. In a tribunal, a request for specific disclosure can be made at any time but a tribunal will frequently be more interested in such an applic-ation if standard disclosure has been ordered at a case management hearing or by an initial order and the requested documents were not produced.

(h) Regulatory proceedings, such as through the GMC or NMC. These proceedings are outside the scope of this book but are sometimes seen in overlap with a dispute that is heard in a court or tribunal. Those within the GMC may wish to consult the 2015 review by Sir Anthony Hooper, a retired Court of Appeal judge, into "The handling by the General Medical Council of cases involving whistleblowers", freely available online.

Freedom to Speak Up: raising concerns (whistleblowing) policy for the NHS

This national policy aims to standardise the treatment of how whistleblowing is treated and expressly aims to contribute "to the need to develop a more open and supportive culture that encourages staff to raise any issues of patient care quality or safety", with an opening heading of "speak up – we will listen" (p.3). The policy is available on the NHS Improvement website[1], wherein it is stated:

"Our policy will ensure:

- NHS organisations encourage staff to speak up and set out the steps they will take to get to the bottom of any concerns

- organisations will each appoint their own whistleblowing guardian, an independent and impartial source of advice to staff at any stage of raising a concern

---

1 https://improvement.nhs.uk/resources/freedom-to-speak-up-whistleblowing-policy-for-the-nhs/

- any concerns not resolved quickly through line managers are investigated

- investigations will be evidence-based and led by someone suitably independent in the organisation, producing a report which focuses on learning lessons and improving care

- whistleblowers will be kept informed of the investigation's progress

- high level findings are provided to the organisation's board and the policy will be annually reviewed and improved

We expect all NHS organisations in England to adopt this policy as a minimum standard to help to normalise the raising of concerns for the benefit of all patients."

The 10-page policy applies to a wide range of NHS staff, answering "who can raise concerns?" with broad non-exhaustive examples of "agency workers, temporary workers, students, volunteers and governors" (p.5). It further details the role of the Speak Up Guardian, who should be identified to staff as the person overseeing the raising and treatment of concerns by NHs staff. The policy states they are "an independent and impartial source of advice to staff at any stage of raising a concern, with access to anyone in the organisation, including the chief executive, or if necessary, outside the organisation" (p.5). The policy is non-committal in its description of the practical and detailed steps that will be part of an investigation, stating that there will be "a proportionate investigation" and "we will reach a conclusion with a reasonable timescale" (p.6). The lack of detail here is intentional as the policy allows for integration with an NHS employer's local policy and highlights the need to link to that local policy so that workers are clear on the individual procedure that is applied by their employer.

A claim in the employment tribunal

For some, the internal raising of their concern will lead to a satisfactory investigation or at least a record of the issue and they will feel no need to take further action. Others feel that as a result of raising their concern they are targeted and suffer. In such a case, an employment tribunal claim is a potential. The most common types of claim in a tribunal are that as a result of one or more protected disclosures, the whistleblower has been dismissed (contrary to s.103A ERA 1996) or has suffered a detriment (contrary to s.47B ERA 1996). These two claims will be the focus of this book and therefore references will be to a tribunal rather than a court.

A claim pursuant to either s.103A or s.47B ERA is technical and a significant number of requirements are prescribed by legislation. The correct statutory boxes have to be ticked. The most significant piece of legislation that introduced the statutory definitions is the Public Interest Act 1998 ("PIDA 1998"), but in practice this is utilised by its implementation into the Employment Rights Act 1996 ("ERA 1996") and in particular Parts IVA and V. The chapters that follow address the key issues that arise from the statutory requirements, broadly considering whether a protected disclosure has actually been made and whether there was a detriment or dismissal as a result. In this chapter some key practical issues that arise when an employment tribunal claim is issued will be considered.

The start of a tribunal claim

When a claim is started with an ET1 form, the precise and detailed statutory requirements of the protected disclosure regime should all be set out. It is regrettably common in practice for parties to have to attend a preliminary hearing (PH) so that the claimant can flesh out the detail of the claim they are making, particularly on the issue of how the Claimant alleges that a disclosure was made. Partly for this reason, PHs are discussed in their own further section below. Those drafting the ET1 or an attached Grounds of Complaint would do well to cross reference their draft against the legislation, particularly s.43B that sets out the definition of a qualifying disclosure, to try and ensure that the required facts are stated. The remaining chapters in this book give detail about the legislative details that need to be identified.

The need to explain the factual matters relied upon was highlighted by the Court of Appeal in *Kilraine v London Borough of Wandsworth* [2018] EWCA Civ 1436. In highlighting that the "information" disclosed by a purported protected disclosure should be assessed in the light of the particular context in which it is made, the CoA at para. 41 highlighted the need for the context to be explained in the ET1 and the purpose of enabling the Respondent to fairly understand and respond:

> "If such a disclosure was to be relied upon for the purposes of a whistleblowing claim under the protected disclosures regime in Part IVA of the ERA, the meaning of the statement to be derived from its context should be explained in the claim form and in the evidence of the claimant so that it is clear on what basis the worker alleges that he has a claim under that regime. The employer would then have a fair opportunity to dispute the context relied upon, or whether the oral statement could

really be said to incorporate by reference any part of the factual background in this manner."

Time Limits

The time limits for a Claimant to make a claim that as a result of a protected disclosure they have suffered a detriment or been dismissed are set out by s.48(3) and s.111(2) ERA 1996 respectively.

Firstly, in respect of detriment claims, s.48(3) prescribes:

"(3) An [employment tribunal] shall not consider a complaint under this section unless it is presented—

(a) before the end of the period of three months beginning with the date of the act or failure to act to which the complaint relates or, where that act or failure is part of a series of similar acts or failures, the last of them, or

(b) within such further period as the tribunal considers reasonable in a case where it is satisfied that it was not reasonably practicable for the complaint to be presented before the end of that period of three months.

(4) For the purposes of subsection (3)—

(a) where an act extends over a period, the "date of the act" means the last day of that period, and

(b) a deliberate failure to act shall be treated as done when it was decided on;

and, in the absence of evidence establishing the contrary, an employer[, a temporary work agency or a hirer] shall be taken to decide on a failure to act when he does an act inconsistent with doing the failed act or, if he has done no such inconsistent act, when the period expires within which he might reasonably have been expected do the failed act if it was to be done."

For many acts or failures to act, the date on which they occurred will be easy to understand and the above statement applied. Complications are more likely to arise when considering if acts or failures are "part of a series of similar acts or failures" and it is important that parties and tribunals "should not confuse a continuing detriment with a continuing act (or cause)" (para. 33 of *Royal Mail Group Ltd v Jhuti* [2018] UKEAT 0020_16_1903 (19 March 2018, Unreported). In *Jhuti*, the EAT allowed an appeal where it was held that the tribunal had confused acts with detrimental consequences because the tribunal had erroneously held that a series of acts was in time as a result of confusing the in-time consequences of an out of time act with the act itself, highlighting "That the earlier acts had continuing detrimental consequences is irrelevant for time purposes" (para. 47). The EAT further highlighted the simple point that when considering if there is a series of acts that is in time, at least one must succeed as a claim, "there must be at least one in-time proven act that infringes the relevant provision" (para. 45). *Jhuti* was later appealed in the CoA but these points from the EAT remain undisturbed (and at the time of writing it is expected to be heard again in the Supreme Court in 2019).

Knowledge of the detriment is not required for time limits to commence. "Time runs from the date of the 'act' regardless of whether a claimant has any knowledge of the detriment that the act produces: see *Flynn v Warrior Square Recoveries Ltd* [2014] EWCA Civ 68 and *McKinney v Newham London BC* [2015] ICR 495", from *Jhuti* EAT para. 32. This contrasts with the position regarding dismissal, in which case in the absence of a specific contractual provision, notice will take effect when it is received by the employee and they have read it, or had a reasonable opportunity to do so. Note though that this position was analysed by the Supreme Court in detail in *Newcastle upon Tyne NHS Foundation Trust v Haywood* [2018] UKSC 22 and the complexities are demonstrated by the 3-2 split of the UK's highest national court.

For a dismissal claim, the primary time limit at s.111 ERA is in very similar language to that for a detriment claim outlined above, substituting the act or failure to act for "the effective date of termination". The effective date of termination ("EDT") will often be easy to determine and is effectively the date on which the dismissal takes effect. Each case is fact dependent but as generalisations, if there is a dismissal without notice the EDT will likely be on the date on which the dismissal decision was communicated and if notice is provided and served, the EDT will likely be at the end of that period of notice. Complications can arise in these examples, particularly if notice is required but not served. The statutory definition of the EDT at s.97 ERA 1996 should be consulted if there is any ambiguity.

The time limits for both a detriment and dismissal claim are subject to the 'extension' regime of the **ACAS Early Conciliation** ("EC") procedure, pursuant to s.48(4A) ERA and s.111(2A) ERA respectively. Nearly all claims within a tribunal, whistleblowing or otherwise, must begin by going through the ACAS EC procedure contained principally in the Employment Tribunals Act 1996 and implemented at s.207B ERA 1996 for the purposes of an unfair dismissal or detriment claim and within other relevant legislation where applicable.

Broadly, the EC procedure forces the parties into a period of conciliation, which can last from 1 day to 6 weeks but typically lasts one month, and the end of the period is marked by the issuing of the ACAS EC certificate. The time limit is extended by either the time spent in the EC regime or one month, but a detailed consideration of the procedure is outside of the scope of this book.

Another important parallel between the two time limits is the test for when a claim is issued out of time, in both cases requiring an assessment of whether issuing in time was "**not reasonably practicable**" for the Claimant to have issued in time and whether they issued within a "reasonable" period after the expiry of the time limit. Both parts have to be satisfied and the burden is on the Claimant to show that it was not reasonably practicable to have issued in time, per para. 28 of *Marks & Spencer v Williams-Ryan* [2005] IRLR 562 and *Porter v Banbridge Ltd* [1978] IRLR 271.

"not reasonably practicable" is a narrower test than the "just and equitable" test for seeking an extension under other legislation, notably the Equality Act 2010. It has been equated to a test of "reasonable feasibility" Palmer and Saunders v Southend-on-Sea Borough Council [1984] 1 All ER 945.

Ignorance of the time limit is a factor considered by many cases but one that may be increasingly hard for Claimants to rely upon in today's information saturated society, with information on time limits provided from various sources, notably the internet and guidance from organisations such as ACAS. A "generous" (but not perverse) finding by an employment tribunal, in the words of the Court of Appeal, was seen in *Williams-Ryan* in which the Claimant's ignorance of a time limit was successful in demonstrating that it was not reasonably practicable because she had been giving misleading advice by her employer. The Court of Appeal observed of 'ignorance' cases at para. 21:

> "regard should be had to what, if anything, the employee knew about the right to complain to the employment tribunal and of the time limit for making such a complaint. Ignorance of either

does not necessarily render it not reasonably practicable to bring a complaint in time. It is necessary to consider not merely what the employee knew, but what knowledge the employee should have had had he or she acted reasonably in all the circumstances."

Defective actions of legal advisers also typically carries little weight if a time limit is missed, with Claimants often being fixed with the mistake of their advisers and left to pursue the adviser if worthwhile. In *Wall's Meat Co Ltd v Khan* [1978] IRLR 499, a case examining this test in detail especially on the subject of ignorance, it was observed by Lord Denning of the role of advisers:

"Ignorance of his rights – or ignorance of the time limit – is not just cause or excuse, unless it appears that he or his advisers could not reasonably be expected to have been aware of them. If he or his advisers could reasonably have been so expected, it was his or their fault, and he must take the consequences."

However, there is no absolute rule that a mistake of an adviser relied upon will always mean that a Claimant cannot claim it was not reasonably practicable to have issued in time, see the analysis of Underhill P (as he then was) in *Northamptonshire County Council v Entwhistle* [2010] IRLR 740 at para. 9.

Underhill P developed this analysis in the context of the second limb of the test, i.e. whether the claim was issued within in a reasonable period, in *Cullinane v Balfour Beatty Engineering Services Limited* (UKEAT/0537/10, Unreported, April 2011), observing of the second limb at para. 16:

"That is not the same as asking whether the claimant acted reasonably; still less is it equivalent to the question whether it would be just and equitable to extend time. It requires an objective consideration of the factors causing the delay and what period should reasonably be allowed in those circumstances for proceedings to be instituted – having regard, certainly, to the strong public interest in claims in this field being brought promptly, and against a background where the primary time limit is three months. If a period is, on that basis, objectively unreasonable, I do not see how the fact that the delay was caused by the claimant's advisers rather than by himself can make any difference to that conclusion."

Preliminary Hearings

There are broadly two types of preliminary hearing (PH), those that deal with case management and those that deal with substantive issues. The two can be combined.

Case management of protected disclosure claims is often required to ensure that the Claimant has adequately addressed all of the relevant statutory requirements. As above, this can be best avoided by cross-referencing the legislation to the grounds of complaint before they are finalised. If a PH is needed, this can be determined by the tribunal of its own initiative or applied for by the parties, including by the Respondent in its Grounds of Resistance, although a separate formal application may be more efficient. At a PH, a Claimant unable to address the relevant statutory requirements may be given a chance to provide further and better particulars, typically provided with at least 14 days, and a Respondent may then be allowed a chance to respond to those if so advised, again typically provided with at least 14 days thereafter.

Protected disclosure claims can also be appropriate for a PH determining a substantive issue. The detailed prescriptions of the protected disclosure regime mean that if the required statutory boxes are not ticked for one issue, the whole claim may fall away. For example, questions over whether a protected disclosure has been made or whether a person is a worker may be discreet issues that can be determined with evidence at a PH. If the Claimant is unsuccessful, the whole claim or a major part may fall away and this will save the parties and tribunal time, expense and resources. Such a PH may be particularly suitable when the disclosures are in writing because the determination of whether they tick the right statutory boxes to constitute protected disclosures should not require much evidence beyond the documents themselves.

On the other hand, if there is little resource saving because, for example, a question of unfair dismissal remains and the claim of dismissal due to a protected disclosure only adds on a small amount of time to consider motivation, a PH may not be suitable. Similarly, a PH may be unsuitable if there is significant factual dispute over an oral disclosure or a Claimant's argument that detailed factual context is essential to understanding the disclosure (as in *Bolton School v Evans* [2006] IRLR 500, for example).

Again, a PH dealing with a substantive issue could be requested in the Grounds of Resistance or in anticipation of or at a case management PH. They are typically not requested by Claimants, but it is fully open to a Claimant to make such a request if, for example, seeking an early determination of a fundamental issue rather than pursue their claim if they fear losing after expending much time and money. Alternatively, a PH may be suggested by the Tribunal of its own initiative. In *Kilraine*, for example, the Court of Appeal record that at the employment tribunal after proceeding all the way to trial, following a delayed start to the trial the tribunal had pre-read the witness statements then identified the issue of whether a protected disclosure had been made and suggested this as a preliminary issue to be determined at the outset, perhaps motivated here by the lost time at the start. Evidence of some degree will be needed, albeit this may only comprise the relevant written documentation if the disclosures were in writing, a focused witness statement from the Claimant and perhaps no evidence from the Respondent if they can add nothing to the issue.

Beyond the specifics of a discreet substantive issue, there may also be a PH to consider a strikeout or deposit order. Certainly for a strike out, a determination against a Claimant will have the same effect as the determination of a substantive issue against a Claimant by ending the claim. Parties contemplating or faced with such a PH should consider the extensive case law on strike out orders, much of which emphasises that there is a high threshold to meet. See for example, Lady Smith's summary in *Balls v Downham Market High School and College* [2011] IRLR 217 that it was, "in short, a high test", the warning against strike outs when there is a material dispute of facts in *North Glamorgan NHS Trust v Ezsias* [2007] IRLR 603 and the direction by Langstaff J sitting as the President of the EAT in *Day v Lewisham and Greenwich NHS Trust and another* [2016] IRLR 415 at para. 10:

> "when considering whether to strike out a claim a Tribunal must accept the facts asserted by the Claimant in his originating application, taken at their reasonable highest in his favour"

The similar approach to a deposit order is outlined by Simler J, succeeding as President of the EAT, in *Hemdan v Ishmail* [2017] IRLR 228 at paras. 12 and 13.

Evidence

Clearly each case will be determined by its own facts and tribunals are therefore likely to be resistant to placing much weight on broad assertions or generalisations based on wide data rather than evidence specific to the individual case. Guidance on what evidence can be persuasive for either a Claimant or Respondent is therefore difficult to provide, but the following sources may in certain cases provide useful information, some of which can be found online or may have to be requested:

- Summary Hospital-level Mortality Indicator data (SHMI) – this provides the ratio between the number of patients who die following hospitalisation at a trust and the number that would be expected to die on the basis of average figures for England, considering the characteristics of the patients treated there and including deaths occurring in hospital and outside within 30 days of discharge.

- Hospital Standardised Mortality Ration data (HSMR) – similarly, a ratio indicating a comparison to expected deaths based on national scoring.

- The Dr Foster Unit – based at Imperial College London, the Unit is heavily involved in the analysis of statistical data involving the NHS, particularly concerning issues of patient safety.

- A Freedom of Information Request – a request made pursuant to the 2000 Act that should entitle an individual to obtain recorded information held by a public authority, including the NHS. Relevant information could include, for example, the number of concerns raised about a certain issue or the number of times a certain action has been taken such as application of the whistleblowing policy. The information provided may include the actual documents, files or correspondence. If a Claimant seeks personal data about themselves, an SAR request, below, should be made instead.

- A 'Subject Access Request' is often used by a Claimant to gain disclosure ahead of the tribunal process, requesting effectively all information held about or referring to them as an individual. Since May 2018, this is made pursuant to the GDPR and a response should generally be received within one month and no fee charged by the employer.

- The final chapter of this book outlines various organisations that focus on whistleblowing from both parties' perspectives and who may be able to assist in the collation of evidence.

CHAPTER TWO
WHO CAN BE A WHISTLEBLOWER?

'Whistleblower' is not a term used by statute. Instead, a person who makes a protected disclosure is who statute defines and commonly such a person is often referred to as a whistleblower. This chapter will look at the category of people that statute deems eligible to make a protected disclosure and who can therefore rely upon the protection of PIDA 1998. The definitions or worker and employee will be considered, as well as new regulations specific to job applicants.

Like much of statutory employment law, a Claimant is only able to make a claim in a tribunal to seek the protection of PIDA 1998 if they satisfy the applicable legislative criteria. Two categories apply: workers and employees. Both can make a protected disclosure pursuant to s.43A ERA 1996 and both can bring a claim that they have suffered a detriment as a result pursuant to s.48(1A) ERA 1996, but only an employee can bring a claim that they have been dismissed as a result of a protected disclosure pursuant to s.103A ERA 1996. A worker who wants to claim about their dismissal may nevertheless be able to claim a very similar remedy as if they had made a claim under s.103A ERA 1996, as discussed below in the Liability chapter.

For many, their status will be easily identified, uncontroversial and it will be identified in their contract. Arguments over employment status emerge when the individual is not expressly identified as a worker or employee but claim to be one of these to avail themselves of statutory protection.

Worker in this context is defined in two places: s. 230 ERA 1996 and s.43K ERA 1996.

s.230 ERA 1996 provides:

"s.230 Employees, workers etc

(1) In this Act "employee" means an individual who has entered into or works under (or, where the employment has ceased, worked under) a contract of employment.

(2) In this Act "contract of employment" means a contract of service or apprenticeship, whether express or implied, and (if it is express) whether oral or in writing.

(3) In this Act "worker" (except in the phrases "shop worker" and "betting worker") means an individual who has entered into or works under (or, where the employment has ceased, worked under)—

(a) a contract of employment, or

(b) any other contract, whether express or implied and (if it is express) whether oral or in writing, whereby the individual undertakes to do or perform personally any work or services for another party to the contract whose status is not by virtue of the contract that of a client or customer of any profession or business undertaking carried on by the individual;

and any reference to a worker's contract shall be construed accordingly.

(4) In this Act "employer", in relation to an employee or a worker, means the person by whom the employee or worker is (or, where the employment has ceased, was) employed.

(5) In this Act "employment"—

(a) in relation to an employee, means (except for the purposes of section 171) employment under a contract of employment, and

(b) in relation to a worker, means employment under his contract;

and "employed" shall be construed accordingly.

[(6) This section has effect subject to sections 43K[, 47B(3) *and 49B(10)*] [,_49B(10) and 49C(12)]; and for the purposes of Part XIII so far as relating to Part IVA or section 47B, "worker", "worker's contract" and, in relation to a worker, "employer", "employment" and "employed" have the extended meaning given by section 43K.]..."

s.230(3)(a) covers employees, giving them the additional status of workers.

s.230(3)(b) has proven to be a lot more controversial and in the raft of case law that has developed to consider its meaning, employment status pursuant to this category is "conveniently described as a limb (b) worker" (*Pimlico Plumbers Ltd & Anor v Smith* [2018] UKSC 29). Much of the recent case law in this area has emerged from disputes from individuals with a lot of flexibility in their work and from issues from the 'gig economy' and zero hour contracts etc. The detail of this area is not explored here because of the more relevant application of s.43K ERA 1996, but recent and authoritative guidance can be gleamed from the June 2018 judgment of the Supreme Court in *Pimlico Plumbers* and the SC's previous observations in *Bates van Winkelhof v Clyde& Co LLP* [2014] UKSC 32 and *Autoclenz Ltd v Belcher* [2011] UKSC 41.

s.43K ERA 1996 is a section created only for whistleblowing claims and it expressly extends the meaning of worker beyond s.230 in certain circumstances, therefore broadening the protection available. It provides:

"43K Extension of meaning of "worker" etc for Part IVA]

[(1) For the purposes of this Part "worker" includes an individual who is not a worker as defined by section 230(3) but who—

(a) works or worked for a person in circumstances in which—

(i) he is or was introduced or supplied to do that work by a third person, and

(ii) the terms on which he is or was engaged to do the work are or were in practice substantially determined not by him but by the person for whom he works or worked, by the third person or by both of them,

(b) contracts or contracted with a person, for the purposes of that person's business, for the execution of work to be done in a place not under the control or management of that person and would fall within section 230(3)(b) if for "personally" in that provision there were substituted "(whether personally or otherwise)",

[(ba) works or worked as a person performing services under a contract entered into by him with [the National Health Service Commissioning Board] [under [section 83(2), 84, 92, 100, 107, 115(4), 117 or 134 of, or Schedule 12 to,] the National Health Service Act 2006 or with a Local Health Board under [section 41(2)(b), 42, 50, 57, 64 or 92 of, or Schedule 7 to,] the National Health Service (Wales) Act 2006]. . .,] [(bb) works or worked as a person performing services under a contract entered into by him with a Health Board under section 17J [or 17Q] of the National Health Service (Scotland) Act 1978,]

(c) [works or worked as a person providing services] in accordance with arrangements made—

(i) by [the National Health Service Commissioning Board] [[under section 126 of the National Health Service Act 2006,] or] [Local Health Board] under [section 71 or 80 of the National Health Service (Wales) Act 2006], or

(ii) by a Health Board under section [2C, 17AA, 17C,] . . . 25, 26 or 27 [or 26] of the National Health Service (Scotland) Act 1978, . . .

[(ca) . . .]

[(cb) is or was provided with work experience provided pursuant to a course of education or training approved by, or under arrangements with, the Nursing and Midwifery Council in accordance with article 15(6)(a) of the Nursing and Midwifery Order 2001 (SI 2002/253), or]

(d) is or was provided with work experience provided pursuant to a training course or programme or with training for employment (or with both) otherwise than—

(i) under a contract of employment, or

(ii) by an educational establishment on a course run by that establishment;

and any reference to a worker's contract, to employment or to a worker being "employed" shall be construed accordingly...."

s.43K(1)(a) has proven to be the most controversial. Its reference to being "introduced or supplied to do that work by a third person" means it will be relevant to agency workers and other similar individuals placed to work in the NHS by a third party. The section and particularly the reference to terms being "substantially determined not by him but by the person for whom he works or worked, by the third person or by both of them" was considered by the Court of Appeal in *Day v Health Education England & Ors* [2017] EWCA Civ 329. Dr Day was a worker of Lewisham and Greenwich NHS Trust but he also claimed to be a worker of Health Education England due to the organisation of his training. The Court of Appeal considered whether his status as a worker for the Trust precluded him from also being a worker within s.43K of HEE because he claimed HEE had caused him detriments, holding that the dual status was no bar to claiming PIDA protection. Elias LJ highlighted various factors that influenced his view (paras. 15-21), including that this would allow him to have protection against the end-user as well as the introducer.

The conclusion was "reinforced" due to an earlier decision of Simler J sitting then as the President of the EAT in *McTigue v University Hospital Bristol NHS Trust* [2016] ICR 1156, a case in which your author appeared for the Claimant. As stated by Elias LJ, "that case raised the question whether an end user in an agency arrangement was an employer within the meaning of the extended definition in section 43K" (para. 22) and in answering in the affirmative, Simler J highlighted "an important purpose of s.43K is to extend cover to agency workers in relation to victimisation for protected disclosures made while working at the end user" (para. 27).

Status as an 'employee' is defined at s.230(1), quoted above. The definition essentially denotes an individual engaged "under a contract of employment". Unsurprisingly, the simplicity of this definition has led to much discussion in case law, too lengthy and not necessary for the purposes of this book. For useful guidance, see *Autoclenz, Windle v Secretary of State for Justice* [2016] ICR 721 and *Cox v Ministry of Justice* [2016] UKSC 10.

Whatever status an individual holds, a disclosure made via a third party may still constitute a protected disclosure despite not being made directly from the individual. In *Cavendish Munro Professional Risks Management Ltd v. Geduld* [2010] ICR 325, discussed in greater length in the next chapter, the disclosure was made in a letter sent by the Claimant's solicitors to his employer. Although the disclosure was held not to be a protected disclosure for other reasons, no problem was seen by the tribunal or EAT due to the Claimant making the disclosure via a third party. How far this principle can extend to other agents of an individual remains to be tested and it may be that solicitors are seen as a clearer and more direct voice of their client than other agents, such as a work colleague or even trade union who may not be 'instructed' in the same way.

Beyond s.43K(1)(a), the remaining sub-sections of s.43K are largely fact specific and depend on whether or not the individual has the stipulated contract or relationship with the NHS or related organisation. The sub-sections are intentionally wide in their remit and the combined effect of s.43K(1)(a) will likely incorporate the vast majority of those engaged in some form within the NHS.

NHS Job Applicants

The 2015 Freedom to Speak Up review (discussed in more detail in the final chapter) concluded its chapter on Extending Legal Protection with one emphatic need for improved protection because it found that, "individuals are suffering, or are at risk of suffering, serious detriments in seeking re-employment in the health service after making a protected disclosure" (para. 9.19). After consultation, the report's recommendation resulted in the Employment Rights Act 1996 (NHS Recruitment – Protected Disclosure) Regulations 2018. These Regulations came into force in May 2018.

As discussed further in relation to 'who to claim against' in the Liability chapter, a whistleblower does not have to have raised a concern to the Respondent against whom they seek protection (see also *BP v (1) Elstone (2) Petrotechnics* [2010] IRLR 558, which highlighted that a "straightforward reading of the words of the statute" (para. 33) denotes that a whistleblower can in theory make a protected disclosure against one employer and then later seek protection from another employer on the basis of the earlier disclosure).

Job applicants however, may be left without protection from their new prospective employer because they will not be the new employer's worker at the point of application (see the discussion of this potential "lacuna" at *Elstone* para. 37). For NHS job applicants, the 2018 Regulations therefore seek to obviate this problem. The Regulations make this protection express in the context of NHS employers (as defined by Reg.2 and s.49B ERA 1996) and go further by not requiring the applicant to have actually made a protected disclosure, but affording protection under Reg.3 in a broader sense based on perception:

"Prohibition of discrimination because of protected disclosure

3. An NHS employer must not discriminate against an applicant because it appears to the NHS employer that the applicant has made a protected disclosure."

If there has been discrimination, an applicant can apply to an employment tribunal under Reg.4 and obtain a declaration under

Reg.6, "just and equitable" compensation under Regs. 6-7 and a recommendation for action to obviate or reduce the effect of the discrimination under Reg.6. There is a further opportunity to apply for a court for action and damages "which may include compensation for injured feelings" at Reg.8, discussed below.

The time limit within an employment tribunal for bringing a claim is 3 months, starting from a range of dates depending on the category of action taken by the prospective employer and including an express provision that in the case of a decision not to employ or appoint an applicant that the 3 months begins on "the date that decision was communicated to the applicant" (Reg.5(3)(a)). Any extension to this time limit is under the "just and equitable" test familiar from the EA 2010.

Borrowing further from the legislative regime in discrimination law, the burden of proof at Reg.4(2) provides:

> "If there are facts from which the employment tribunal could decide, in the absence of any other explanation, that an NHS employer contravened regulation 3, the tribunal must find that such a contravention occurred unless the NHS employer shows that it did not contravene regulation 3."

Further familiar statutory provisions are in the express statement of vicarious liability at Reg.9(1), as well as the potential defence for a respondent at Reg.9(4) if they can demonstrate they took all reasonable steps to prevent a worker or agent from carrying out the discrimination or anything of that description.

The wide scope of remedies at Reg.8 will be unfamiliar to some employment law practitioners because it envisages a remedy in a County Court or High Court. The potential at Reg.8(3)(a) for "such order as [the court] considers appropriate for the purpose of restraining or preventing the defendant from contravening regulation 3" is most likely to be relied upon for an injunction, such as restraining the appointment of an alternative candidate or ordering a fresh recruitment exercise with new decision makers. Concern was expressed during consultation about the burden on respondents having to defend two sets of proceedings, i.e. one in the employment tribunal and one in a civil court, but Reg.8(4)-(5) aims to obviate this difficulty:

> "(4) Except as provided in paragraph (5), an applicant may not complain to an employment tribunal under regulation 4 and bring an action for breach of statutory duty in respect of the same conduct.

> (5) An applicant may complain to an employment tribunal under regulation 4 and bring an action for breach of statutory duty in respect of the same conduct for the purpose of restraining or pre-venting the defendant from contravening regulation 3."

CHAPTER THREE
HAS THE WHISTLE BEEN
BLOWN?

This chapter moves on to consider the fundamental question of whether a protected disclosure has been made and then looks at the procedure through which this is determined. The chapter outlines the extensive statutory requirements that must all be satisfied in order for the whistleblowing protection to be used and highlights some of the nuances of the legislative provisions. Broadly, the two requirements for the right content and the right audience for a protected disclosure will be considered.

As with the question of 'who is a whistleblower?', there are detailed and specific statutory requirements that must be satisfied in order to rely upon the relevant legislation. If a claim does not tick all of the correct statutory boxes, it will not succeed. Raising a concern that is not a protected disclosure may be labelled as a 'complaint', a 'grievance' or even a 'moan', but if it does not count as a protected disclosure the protection of PIDA 1998 cannot be relied upon in a court or tribunal. Similarly, an NHS employer may legitimately decline to treat a concern under their whistleblowing policy if the concern is not a protected disclosure and instead is better treated as a grievance and therefore potentially require a less extensive investigation, for example, but this would of course have to consider the specific policies concerned.

In a tribunal, the initial burden is on the Claimant to demonstrate that a protected disclosure has been made and the right statutory boxes have been ticked, see *Boulding v Land Securities Trillium (Media Services) Ltd* (UKEAT/0023/06, *Unreported, 3 May 2006*).

For the question of whether a protected disclosure has been made, there are broadly two considerations:

1. Does the protected disclosure contain the required *content*?

2. Has the protected disclosure been made in the required *manner*?

These two questions mirror the start of the PIDA legislation as it is incorporated into Part IVA Employment Rights Act 1996 ("ERA 1996") at s.43A ERA 1996 (inserted by s.1 PIDA 1998):

"s. 43A Meaning of 'Protected Disclosure'

In this Act a "protected disclosure" means a qualifying disclosure (as defined by section 43B) which is made by a worker in accordance with any of sections 43C to 43H."

s.43A states that for there to be a protected disclosure, there must first be a qualifying disclosure (defined at s.43B ERA 1996 and covering the question of content) and secondly the qualifying disclosure must have been made in accordance with ss.43C-43H ERA 1996 (covering the question of manner).

The answers to the above two questions are often pivotal to a protected disclosure claim and can therefore result in a request for early determination at a preliminary hearing, as discussed under the chapter on Points of Procedure. For a claim to succeed, each question must be answered in a way that satisfies the legislation and each will now be considered in turn.

Does the disclosure contain the required content?

If the content does not tick the required statutory boxes, the disclosure is not a 'qualifying disclosure' and the legislation cannot be relied upon. The required statutory boxes for content are at s.43B ERA 1996:

"43B Disclosures qualifying for protection

[(1) In this Part a "qualifying disclosure" means any disclosure of information which, in the reasonable belief of the worker making the disclosure, [is made in the public interest and] tends to show one or more of the following—

(a) that a criminal offence has been committed, is being committed or is likely to be committed,

(b) that a person has failed, is failing or is likely to fail to comply with any legal obligation to which he is subject,

(c) that a miscarriage of justice has occurred, is occurring or is likely to occur,

(d) that the health or safety of any individual has been, is being or is likely to be endangered,

(e) that the environment has been, is being or is likely to be damaged, or

(f) that information tending to show any matter falling within any one of the preceding paragraphs has been, or is likely to be deliberately concealed.

[...]"

There are many elements of a disclosure's content that together are required to make the disclosure a qualifying disclosure. Each must be satisfied for the PIDA protection to be relied upon and will now be considered in turn.

For the Respondent's part, there is no requirement that the Respondent itself has to believe that a disclosure was protected within the meaning of the Act:

> "Parliament has enacted a careful and elaborate set of conditions governing whether a disclosure is to be treated as a protected disclosure. It seems to me inescapable that the intention was that the question whether those conditions were satisfied in a given case should be a matter for objective determination by a tribunal; yet if [Counsel] were correct the only question that could ever arise (at least in a dismissal case) would be whether the employer *believed* that they were satisfied. Such a state of affairs would not only be very odd in itself but would be unacceptable in policy terms. It would enormously reduce the scope of the protection afforded by these provisions if liability under section 103A could only arise where the employer itself believed that the disclosures for which the claimant was being dismissed were protected. In many or most cases the employer will not turn his mind to the question whether the disclosure is protected at all. Even where he does, most often he will be convinced, human nature being what it is, that one or more circumstances are present that mean that the disclosure is unprotected"

– *Beatt v Croydon Health Services NHS Trust* [2017] EWCA Civ 401, original emphasis, para. 80

Information

The requirement for information is an important point for NHS whistleblowing cases because concerns are routinely raised through varying degrees of formality and content. There may well be a gulf in detail and emphasis between an oral comment made to a manager in the corridor expressing a concern and the contents of a written Datix entry/clinical incident form submitted on the ward. To rely upon the PIDA protection though, sufficient factual content and specificity must be used for the protected disclosure to be classified as "information" and therefore the content and context of what was disclosed will have to be scrutinised.

The most recent analysis of the definition of "information" is by the CoA in a judgment of June 2018, *Kilraine v London Borough of Wandsworth* [2018] EWCA Civ 1436. Much of the reasoning is a consideration of the legal position widely understood previously but explained by the CoA to be erroneous.

Although *Kilraine* does not provide a prescriptive definition of what is "information", the judgment twice states that a disclosure "has to have a sufficient factual content and specificity such as is capable of tending to show one of the matters listed in [s.43B] subsection (1)" (paras. 35 and 36). 'Facts' and 'specifics' are therefore key to providing 'information'.

In addition, the answer to this issue can be assisted by considering other statutory requirements of s.43B, "it is a question which is likely to be closely aligned with the other requirement set out in section 43B(1), namely that the worker making the disclosure should have the reasonable belief that the information he discloses does tend to show one of the listed matters" (para. 36).

Moreover, further insight can be gained from the CoA's analysis of an earlier EAT case, *Cavendish Munro Professional Risks Management Ltd v Geduld* [2010] IRLR 38. *Cavendish Munro* included the following explanation directly applicable to the NHS at para. 24:

> "the ordinary meaning of giving "information" is conveying facts. In the course of the hearing before us, a hypothetical was advanced regarding communicating information about the state of a hospital. Communicating "information" would be "The wards have not been cleaned for the past two weeks. Yesterday, sharps were left lying around". Contrasted with that would be a statement that "you are not complying with Health and Safety requirements". In our view this would be an allegation not information."

This paragraph in particular led to many employment lawyers viewing a dichotomy between 'information' and 'allegation', but the CoA in Kilraine explained "with the benefit of hindsight" that this paragraph of *Cavendish Munro* "was expressed in a way which has given rise to confusion" (para. 34).

The CoA *Kilraine* explained the correct position, "Section 43B(1) should not be glossed to introduce into it a rigid dichotomy between 'information' on the one hand and 'allegations' on the other" (para. 30) and further endorsed the words of Langstaff J when sitting in the EAT in *Kilraine*:

> "The dichotomy between "information" and "allegation" is not one that is made by the statute itself. It would be a pity if Tribunals were too easily seduced into asking whether it was one or the other when reality and experience suggest that very often information and allegation are intertwined. The decision is not decided by whether a given phrase or paragraph is one or rather the other, but is to be determined in the light of the

statute itself. The question is simply whether it is a disclosure of information. If it is also an allegation, that is nothing to the point."

To determine therefore whether information has been conveyed, there should not be a focus on a distinction between information and allegation. An allegation may constitute information (para. 30), but "not every statement involving an allegation will do so" (para. 31). Facts and specifics should be conveyed. These points and the movement between *Cavendish Munro* to *Kilraine* were repeated in the further 2018 case of *Gibson v London Borough of Hounslow & Anor* [2018] (UKEAT 0033_18_2012, Unreported, December 2018).

Finally, *Kilraine* at para. 36 and *Gibson* at para. 28 remind us of the omnipresent guidance from case law, "Whether an identified statement or disclosure in any particular case does meet that standard will be a matter for evaluative judgment by a tribunal in the light of all the facts of the case".

Reasonable belief of the worker

This requirement is an overarching element, applying to the public interest and 'tends to show' elements of the statutory definition of qualifying disclosure. The requirement is twofold and "the definition has both a subjective and an objective element", per *Chesterton Global Ltd v Nurmohamed* [2017] EWCA Civ 979; [2017] IRLR 837) at para. 8, *Babula v Waltham Forest College* [2007] EWCA Civ 174, [2007] ICR 1026 at para.81 and *Kilraine* at para. 36. As is clear from the language of s.43B itself, "The subjective element is that the worker must believe that the information disclosed tends to show one of the six matters listed in sub-section (1). The objective element is that that belief must be reasonable." (*Chesterton*, para. 8).

The **subjective question** of whether the worker held the belief is a matter of fact and is for the tribunal to assess on the individual facts. A tribunal must be satisfied that the worker held the belief that the disclosure was in the public interest at the time they made the disclosure. If the worker only retrospectively believes that the disclosure was in the public interest, this will not be enough.

This point may not be immediately obvious from the statutory language but is clear from various cases, including *Chesterton* at para. 27, *Soh v Imperial College of Science, Technology and Medicine* (UKEAT/0350/14/DM, Unreported) at para. 42 and *Ibrahim v HCA International Ltd* [2018] (UKEAT 0105/18/1309, Unreported, September 2018) at para. 24. However, on the issue of whether a retrospective belief is valid, Underhill LJ in *Chesterton* was careful to differentiate between the worker having the belief in public interest and the reasons why the worker had such a belief, stating at para. 29:

> "Third, the necessary belief is simply that the disclosure is in the public interest. The particular reasons why the worker believes that to be so are not of the essence. That means that a disclosure does not cease to qualify simply because the worker seeks, as not uncommonly happens, to justify it after the event by reference to specific matters which the tribunal finds were not in his head at the time he made it. Of course, if he cannot give credible reasons for why he thought at the time that the disclosure was in the public interest, that may cast doubt on whether he really thought so at all; but the significance is evidential not substantive. Likewise, in principle a tribunal might find that the particular reasons why the worker believed the disclosure to be in the public interest did not reasonably justify his belief, but nevertheless find it to have been reasonable for different reasons which he had not articulated to himself at the time: all that matters is that his (subjective) belief was (objectively) reasonable."

Given the clear focus on public service, an NHS worker may find it easier than those in other professions to demonstrate that they did hold a genuine subjective belief that their disclosure was in the public interest and potentially that it 'tends to show' one of the pre-scribed parts from s.43B(1) ERA 1996.

Public interest does not however have to be the motivation for a pro-tected disclosure. As summarised in *Ibrahim* by HHJ Stacey at para. 24:

> "Whilst the worker must have a genuine and reasonable belief that the disclosure is in the public interest, that does not have to be his or her predominant, or indeed any part of the motive in making it."

Nevertheless, HHJ Stacey also recognised the guidance from *Chesterton* that, "it would be odd if the public interest did not form at least some part of their motivation in making it, but the belief does not in fact have to form any part of the worker's motivation" (para. 25). *Ibrahim* provides a recent analysis of the public interest test, the appeal there failing on this point because the tribunal had simply found against the Claimant on the facts as to whether he had a subjective belief in the public interest element of his disclosure, finding instead that "the Claimant was seeking to protect his per-sonal interest" (para. 26).

The **objective question** of whether the belief was reasonable is again for the tribunal to consider but, as with many other elements of employment law, when assessing this part a tribunal must be careful not to substitute its own view for that of the worker. In *Chesterton* at para. 28, Underhill LJ highlighted the point "hardly moving much further from the obvious" that "as in the case of any other reason-ableness review, that there may be more than one reasonable view as to whether a particular disclosure was in the public interest". The same point must surely apply to the objectivity of whether inform-ation "tends to show" given this must also be in the reasonable belief of the worker. Underhill LJ further expressly rejected the "range of reasonable responses" familiar from an unfair dismissal claim and "the *Wednesbury* approach" as not helpful, instead emphasising that a tribunal may legitimately form its own view of objectivity, that should not be determinative.

Finally, the later case of *Kilraine* at para. 36 explained the reasoning of *Chesterton* and highlighted the overlap between the assessment of reasonableness and whether 'information' was provided:

> "If the worker subjectively believes that the information he dis-closes does tend to show one of the listed matters and the statement or disclosure he makes has a sufficient factual content and specificity such that it is capable of tending to show that listed matter, it is likely that his belief will be a reas-onable belief."

Made in the public interest

The public interest element was introduced by s.17 Enterprise and Regulatory Reform Act 2013. As explained in the introduction to this book, the changes made by the ERRA 2013 apply only to dis-closures made after 25 June 2013 and the previous position is not explained in detail by this book. For an accessible explanation of the pre-ERRA 2013 context, see the judgment by Underhill LJ in *Chesterton* at paras. 5-17, including useful quotation of the parlia-mentary discussion and explanatory notes concerning the change in legislation.

Chesterton is the current authoritative guide to the meaning of "is made in the public interest". As explained above, this element cannot be separated from the consideration of whether it was "in the reasonable belief of the worker" and the points outlined above under the 'reasonable belief' section should be considered.

As a basic application of the statutory language, a disclosure does not have to have been or be in the public interest. The question is instead whether "in the reasonable belief of the worker" the disclosure was made in the public interest. Clearly each case is fact specific but given that nearly all elements of an NHS worker's job involve some element of public interest, an NHS worker will likely find this section relatively easy to satisfy. A detailed consideration of this element of the protected disclosure test may therefore not be necessary in many NHS whistleblowing cases.

Underhill LJ in *Chesterton* declined to give any express breakdown of "in the public interest", instead observing at para. 31:

> "I do not think there is much value in trying to provide any general gloss... Parliament has chosen not to define it, and the intention must have been to leave it to employment tribunals to apply it as a matter of educated impression... The relevant context here is the legislative history explained at paras. 10-13 above. That clearly establishes that the essential distinction is between disclosures which serve the private or personal interest of the worker making the disclosure and those that serve a wider interest."

Chesterton concerned a disclosure made by an employee in their own interest but about which it was argued was also in the public interest because it "serves the (private) interests of other workers as well" (para. 32). Underhill LJ's conclusion at para. 37 was that even if a disclosure:

"relates to a breach of the worker's own contract of employment (or some other matter under section 43B (1) where the interest in question is personal in character), there may nevertheless be features of the case that make it reasonable to regard disclosure as being in the public interest as well as in the personal interest of the worker."

As an example specific to the NHS, Underhill LJ approved an example submitted by Counsel of a doctor working excessive hours. A disclosure complaining about the hours would be in the personal interest of the doctor, as well as their colleagues, but may well also be in the public interest because of the risk to patients created by the hours (paras. 32 and 27).

As further guidance, Underhill LJ noted that the fourfold classification of relevant factors provided by Counsel "may be a useful tool" (para. 37), reproducing them at para. 34:

"(a) the numbers in the group whose interests the disclosure served – see above;

(b) the nature of the interests affected and the extent to which they are affected by the wrongdoing disclosed – a disclosure of wrongdoing directly affecting a very important interest is more likely to be in the public interest than a disclosure of trivial wrongdoing affecting the same number of people, and all the more so if the effect is marginal or indirect;

(c) the nature of the wrongdoing disclosed – disclosure of deliberate wrongdoing is more likely to be in the public interest than the disclosure of inadvertent wrongdoing affecting the same number of people;

(d) the identity of the alleged wrongdoer – as Mr Laddie put it in his skeleton argument, "the larger or more prominent the wrongdoer (in terms of the size of its relevant community, i.e. staff, suppliers and clients), the more obviously should a disclosure about its activities engage the public interest" – though he goes on to say that this should not be taken too far."

'Tends to show'

The list of six categories of information at s.43B(1)(a) to (f) are largely self-explanatory and their meaning should, like most legislation, be gleamed from a common sense and practical application of the statutory language.

A protected disclosure made by a NHS worker is most likely to concern the categories at (a) criminal offence, (b) failure to comply with a legal obligation, (d) endangerment of health safety or (f) deliberate concealment of another category.

'Endangerment of health and safety' at (d) is the most likely category to apply given the NHS' focus on preserving the nation's health and safety. This is a broad category and would cover endangerment to staff as well as patients. Further, it covers a broad range of issues that may lead to endangerment. In *Fincham v. HM Prison Service* (UKEAT 0925/01/1912, Unreported, 2002), the EAT had no difficulty in finding that a reference to "pressure and stress" was a valid protected disclosure, stating at para. 30:

> "We found it impossible to see how a statement that says in terms "I am under pressure and stress" is anything other than a statement that her health and safety is being or at least is likely to be endangered."

'Breach of a legal obligation' at (b) may also be relevant given the extensive regulatory and legislative requirements operating across the NHS. If such a disclosure is relied upon, the breach of legal obligation relied upon must be identified, "albeit not in strict legal language" *Western Union Payment Services UK Ltd v Anastasiou* (UKEAT 0135/13/2102, Unreported, 21 February 2014) at para. 42-43. Context is fundamental though and this may obviate any deficiency if a specific legal obligation is not relied upon, see Bolton School v Evans [2006] IRLR 500. The recent case of *Ibrahim v HCA International Ltd* [2018] (UKEAT 0105/18/1309, Unreported, September 2018) considered the breadth of a legal obligation in the context of an employee who believed that the false blame of others from a private hospital meant that he had to clear his name and in doing so made a disclosure. The EAT held that his disclosure could come within s.43B(1)(b) ERA because this section would cover tortious duties, including defamation and breach of a statutory duty such as those contained in the Defamation Act 2013, and it was held "the Claimant's complaint of damaging false rumours about him that he has breached patient confidentiality is clearly an allegation that he is being defamed" (para. 21). The *Anastasiou* point above was repeated because "he may not have used the word defamation at the time but his allegation was clear in all but name and use of the precise legal terminology", which was sufficient to satisfy s.43B(1)(b) ERA (although the appeal failed on the public interest test, as above).

'Deliberate concealment' at (f) may be a category relied upon by a whistleblower who believes they have already tried to raise their concerns but that they have been ignored or sidelined.

It is important to note that there is no requirement that the disclosure is factually correct. As succinctly stated in *Babula v Waltham Forest College* [2007] EWCA Civ 174, [2007] ICR 1026 at para. 79, "section 43B(1) uses the phrase "tends to show" not "shows". There is, in short, nothing in section 43B(1) which requires the whistleblower to be right". The facts of *Babula* aptly demonstrate this point because an employee disclosed information about what he believed to be an act of criminal incitement to religious hatred, which would fall within head (a) of section 43B (1). There was in fact at the time no such offence, but it was held that the disclosure nonetheless qualified because it was reasonable for the employee to believe that there was. As *Chesterton* further summarises at para.8, "a belief may be reasonable even if it is wrong".

Has the protected disclosure been made in the required manner?

Assuming the content satisfies the statutory requirements, the next requirement is that the disclosure has been made in the correct manner. This is largely a question of making sure the disclosure has been made to the correct recipient.

ss.43C-43H ERA 1996 set out the sections regarding the required manner. They are alternatives and a Claimant needs only to satisfy one to have made a valid protected disclosure.

The most common and simplest category is that of s.43C, "disclosure to employer or other responsible person":

"[(1) A qualifying disclosure is made in accordance with this section if the worker makes the disclosure . . .—

(a) to his employer, or

(b) where the worker reasonably believes that the relevant failure relates solely or mainly to—

(i) the conduct of a person other than his employer, or

(ii) any other matter for which a person other than his employer has legal responsibility,

to that other person.

(2) A worker who, in accordance with a procedure whose use by him is authorised by his employer, makes a qualifying disclosure to a person other than his employer, is to be treated for the purposes of this Part as making the qualifying disclosure to his employer.]"

For most Claimants, including NHS workers, it is straightforward to identify the employer and therefore whether a disclosure has been made to them. If there is a dispute, this will be a question of fact and the myriad of case law on employment status would have to be considered (see the section above concerning who can be a whistleblower and Autoclenz Ltd v Belcher [2011] UKSC 41 and Pimlico Plumbers Ltd and another v Smith [2018] UKSC 29 for analysis by the Supreme Court).

The remaining categories at ss.43D-43H ERA 1996 are much less common in practice but although the legislation is in parts more lengthy, it is easy to understand and application requires a relatively simple application of the statutory language.

s.43F ERA 1996 is the most likely of these remaining categories to be relevant and it concerns "disclosure to prescribed person". The list of prescribed persons is contained in the schedule to the Public Interest Disclosure (Prescribed Persons) Order 2014, SI 2014/2418, as amended. If a disclosure is made to an organisation on the list and the requirements for reasonable belief at s.43F(1)(b) are satisfied, the disclosure will be valid as a protected disclosure. Organisations on the list of prescribed persons that are most likely to be relevant for NHS workers include the General Medical Council, Nurse and Midwifery Council, Care Inspectorate, Care Quality Commission, Health and Care Professions Council, National Guardian's Office (discussed in the final chapter), General Dental Council, General Optical Council, Health Education England and Health Improvement Scotland.

There is understandably no requirement that the recipient of a disclosure themselves believes that a protected disclosure has been made. For discussion by the Court of Appeal, see *Beatt v Croydon Health Services NHS Trust* [2017] EWCA Civ 401 at para. 80 in the context of a disclosure to an employer.

Finally, the EAT confirmed in *Onyango v Berkeley (t/a Berkeley Solicitors)* [2013] ICR D17 that a disclosure made after the employment relationship has ended can be a valid protected disclosure. HHJ Peter Clark's short judgment of 10 paragraphs confirms that because, as paraphrased, "worker and employer are defined in section 230 ERA as those who are or have ceased to be in a contractual relationship of service or core services", a disclosure made by a worker or employee post-dismissal is capable of amounting to a protected disclosure. The reasoning was based in part on *Woodward v Abbey National Plc* [2006] IRLR 677, which confirmed that a detriment suffered after the employment relationship has ended can be the subject of a valid claim.

CHAPTER FOUR
LIABILITY

This chapter will look at the claims available within a tribunal should a whistleblower claim they have suffered because of a protected disclosure. It will principally look at who to claim against and then consider the intricacies of claims that there has been a detriment and a dismissal. The essential issue of causation and the need to prove that an action was caused by a protected disclosure will be an important focus.

Who to claim against?

There are two claims that may be made by a whistleblower in a tribunal specifically about a protected disclosure. Firstly, that the individual has suffered a detriment contrary to s.47B ERA 1996 and secondly that they have been unfairly dismissed contrary to s.103A ERA 1996. The issue of who to claim against is much more complicated for a detriment claim than dismissal.

s.47B ERA 1996 outlines the three possibilities of who to claim against: either against the employer, a colleague or against an agent of the employer.

"s.47B Protected Disclosures

(1) A worker has the right not to be subjected to any detriment by any act, or any deliberate failure to act, by his employer done on the ground that the worker has made a protected disclosure.

(1A) A worker ("W") has the right not to be subjected to any detriment by any act, or any deliberate failure to act, done—

(a) by another worker of W's employer in the course of that other worker's employment, or

(b) by an agent of W's employer with the employer's authority, on the ground that W has made a protected disclosure..."

The first and simplest claim is against the worker's employer. The employer is liable for its own actions under s.47B(1), denoting actions of workers senior enough and with enough authority to be considered 'the employer'.

A further claim is available against the employer due to its vicarious liability for any action done by its workers, made expressly broad by s.47B(1B) and (1C):

"(1B) Where a worker is subjected to detriment by anything done as mentioned in subsection (1A), that thing is treated as also done by the worker's employer.

(1C) For the purposes of subsection (1B), it is immaterial whether the thing is done with the knowledge or approval of the worker's employer."

The effect of ss.47B(1A)(a), (1B) and (1C) and its creation of vicarious liability for "another worker of W's employer" is so wide that the employer is likely to be vicariously liable for any worker of the employer, regardless of seniority. Practitioners will recognise the provisions as "substantially identical" (*Timis & Anor v Osipov & Anor* [2018] EWCA Civ 2321, para. 30) to s.109 Equality Act 2010. The distinction between a claim under s.47B(1) and s.47B(1B) is nevertheless important because only the employer has the s.47B(1D) defence ('took all reasonable steps') to a claim under s.47B(1A)(a), as discussed below.

An alternative claim against a colleague directly for their personal liability is made pursuant to s.47B(1A)(a) ERA 1996 and was considered in detail and comprehensively summarised in *Timis & Anor v Osipov & Anor* [2018] EWCA Civ 2321. This case explains the background to this subsection and the other changes to s.47B that were made by the Enterprise and Regulatory Reform Act 2013, broadening the scope for liability amongst other changes such as the insertion of the public interest test. In *Osipov*, the Claimant was seeking to sue the directors personally of his former employer because the company had gone into liquidation and the individuals had directors' insurance. This case is considered in more detail below with regards to loss caused by a detriment and the case provides a detailed affirmation that it is possible to claim against individuals for detriments, there in the context of acts leading to dismissal.

If a claim is made against more than one individual, as in *Osipov*, consideration should be given to the contribution position between the individual respondents. The issue did not arise in *Osipov* because the individuals were insured but Underhill LJ included as note 4 his observation that:

> "an interesting question might have arisen... since it has been decided at EAT level that the Civil Liability (Contribution) Act 1978 does not apply to proceedings in the ET: see *Sunderland City Council v Brennan* [2011] UKEAT 0286/110, [2012] ICR 1183"

Finally, a detriment claim can be made pursuant to s.47B(1A)(b) against an agent of the employer acting with the employer's authority. This may be important in cases such as discrimination by end-users if the worker is supplied by an employment agency, subcontractors or even suppliers if acting with the required authority. In the NHS, any attempt to distinguish those such as locums and agency workers as not NHS workers is unlikely to be successful but in any event such individuals would likely be covered by this agency subsection. The same principles that apply for a claim against colleagues are likely to apply if suing an agent and, in such scenarios, consideration should be given to s.43K ERA 1996 and the extended definition of worker discussed in the 'who can be a whistleblower' chapter that may result in an agent being the worker's employer in any event.

A Respondent has various **defences** to avoid liability beyond a basic factual dispute over what happened. Firstly, an employer who faces a claim under s.47B(1B) ERA 1996 on the basis of their vicarious liability has a potential defence provided by s.47B(1D):

> "(1D) In proceedings against W's employer in respect of anything alleged to have been done as mentioned in subsection (1A)(a), it is a defence for the employer to show that the employer took all reasonable steps to prevent the other worker —
>
> (a) from doing that thing, or
>
> (b) from doing anything of that description."

Practitioners will recognise this defence as the 'statutory defence' used in discrimination cases pursuant to s.109 EA 2010 and as in that field, establishing this defence will be a matter of fact for the tribunal to assess. If successfully employed by the employer, this will leave an individual co-worker remaining liable if they are also a party (see *Osipov* para. 30(2)).

As explained above, the distinction between a claim against the employer under s.47B(1) and s.47B(1B) is important because of this s.47B(1D) defence. It could be that, for example, a Claim is based on the actions of the actions of the employer's CEO. The employer would likely be liable itself because the employee is senior enough pursuant to s.47B(1) and they would also be vicariously liable under s.47B(1B). If the employer was successful in establishing the s.47B(1D) defence, this would only apply to the vicarious liability imposed by s.47B(1B) and the employer would remain liable under s.47B(1). If however, the claim was based on the actions of the new apprentice rather than the CEO, the employer may not be liable itself under s.47B(1) because the actions may well not be classed as 'the employer' because of the seniority of the apprentice, therefore the claim for vicarious liability under s.47B(1B) and the potential defence would of s.47B(1D) become much more important. For discussion of this point see *Osipov* para. 32 and on the question of how far can one extend the actions of 'the employer' in the context of an unfair dismissal claim, see *Orr v Milton Keynes Council* [2011] 4 All ER 1256 and in particular paras. 19 cf. 60.

A further defence for an employer who is vicariously liable under s.47B(1B) is to challenge whether the actions of the accused colleague were "in the course of that other worker's employment", as required by s.47B(1A)(a). For recent discussion by the Court of Appeal of similar considerations, see *WM Morrison Supermarkets Plc v Various Claimants* [2018] EWCA Civ 2339 in the context of data theft and *Bellman v Northampton Recruitment Ltd* [2018] EWCA Civ 2214 in the context of behaviour at the Christmas party. Caution should be applied to reading across principles of vicarious liability from common law to similar statutory concepts, as per the House of Lords discussion of this point in *Lister v Hesley Hall Ltd* [2001] 2 WLR 1311.

An individual faced with a claim in their personal capacity or as agent has a defence provided by s.47B(1E):

"(1E) A worker or agent of W's employer is not liable by reason of subsection (1A) for doing something that subjects W to detriment if —

(a) the worker or agent does that thing in reliance on a statement by the employer that doing it does not contravene this Act, and

(b) it is reasonable for the worker or agent to rely on the statement.

But this does not prevent the employer from being liable by reason of subsection (1B)."

Again, practitioners will note the overlap with s.110(3) EA 2010 and the determination of this defence will depend on the subjective facts and objective assessment of reasonableness.

Finally, if a claim is made about the act of the dismissal under s.103A ERA 1996, only the employer can be the Respondent. As Underhill LJ observed at the outset of *Osipov*, "only the employer can be liable for unfair dismissal". A Claimant may nevertheless be able to claim against an individual or employer's agent for the same losses, as explained below.

Whatever the identity of the Respondent against whom proceedings are issued, there is no requirement for the relevant protected disclosure to have been made to that Respondent. That is evident from the reference in both s.47B and s.103A ERA 1996 to the generality of the Claimant having "made a protected disclosure" and would otherwise make otiose protection for important cases such as a worker making a protected disclosure to a regulator but then being targeted by their employer and the express right to make a disclosure to those other than one's employer in ss.43C-H ERA 1996. In *BP v*

(1) Elstone (2) Petrotechnics [2010] IRLR 558, a valid disclosure was made before the Claimant was employed by the later Respondent but this did not prevent the Claimant seeking protection based on that earlier protected disclosure. Of course, if the disclosure was not made to the alleged perpetrator of the detriment, there may be an evidential difficulty in proving that the perpetrator knew of and was motivated by the disclosure (see discussion at *Elstone* para. 35).

Detriments

'Detriment'

As explained and quoted above, a claim that a worker has suffered a detriment is made pursuant to ss.47B and 48(1A) ERA 1996. There is no qualifying period of service and a worker can complain of such a detriment from day one.

Detriment is defined objectively and not subjectively, therefore is not determined by solely the worker's personal feelings. In *Shamoon v Chief Constable of the Royal Ulster Constabulary* [2003] 2 All ER 26, Lord Hope explained that the question to be asked when assessing whether there was treatment that amounts to a detriment is, "Is the treatment of such a kind that a reasonable worker would or might take the view that in all the circumstances it was to his detriment?", at para. 35. He further added, "An unjustified sense of grievance cannot amount to 'detriment'...[but] it is not necessary to demonstrate some physical or economic consequence". In particular, "an alleged victim cannot establish detriment merely by showing that she had suffered mental distress" (*St Helens BC v Derbyshire and Others* [2007] UKHL 16, para 68). Although these observations were made in the context of a discrimination claim, the same observations must also be true when looking at 'detriment' within the context of the PIDA legislation.

A detriment suffered after the employment relationship has ended can be the subject of a valid claim, confirmed in *Woodward v Abbey National Plc* [2006] EWCA Civ 822, [2006] IRLR 677. Mrs Woodward brought a claim relating to various post-dismissal acts including failures to provide a reference, progress her job application and respond to a letter and the fact these acts occurred after her dismissal did not prevent them from being potentially valid claims for detriments suffered on the grounds of a protected disclosure. The later case of *Onyango v Berkeley (t/a Berkeley Solicitors)* [2013] ICR D17 similarly confirmed that a disclosure made after the employment relationship has ended can be a valid protected disclosure.

'On the ground that'

If a detriment is established, a tribunal must consider causation and in practice the hurdle of causation can often be the reason that makes or breaks a claim. In *International Petroleum Ltd & Ors v Osipov & Ors* [2017] UKEAT 0058/17/1907, Simler P, as she then was, summarised the principles relating to the burden of proof for causation in a s.47B detriment claim, stating at para.115:

"I agree that the proper approach to inference drawing and the burden of proof in a s.47B ERA 1996 case can be summarised as follows:

(a) the burden of proof lies on a claimant to show that a ground or reason (that is more than trivial) for detrimental treatment to which he or she is subjected is a protected disclosure he or she made.

(b) By virtue of s.48(2) ERA 1996, the employer (or other respondent) must be prepared to show why the detrimental treatment was done. If they do not do so inferences may be drawn against them: see *London Borough of Harrow v. Knight* at paragraph 20.

(c) However, as with inferences drawn in any discrimination case, inferences drawn by tribunals in protected disclosure cases must be justified by the facts as found."

The statement that the ultimate burden rests on a claimant may be seen by some as conflicting with s.48(2) ERA, which outlines a burden on the respondent because "it is for the employer to show the ground on which any act, or deliberate failure to act was done", per s.48(2) ERA 1996. It should be noted that any application of s.48 applies equally to a claim against an employer as it does against an individual colleague or an agent, per s.48(5)(b).

The statement of law approved above by Simler P appears to denote that the overall burden is on the claimant because it is after all their claim, but the claimant may derive assistance in meeting this burden from s.48(2) if the employer cannot provide a satisfactory explanation to why the treatment occurred. It is not simply that the burden is on the respondent.

The approach of the EAT here reflects another decision by Simler P about very similar protection for employees against detriment caused by trade union membership in *Serco Ltd v Dahou [2015] IRLR 30. In a similar point made in para. 115(c) of Osipov above, Simler P stated at para. 53 in Dahou concerning dismissal:*

"if a tribunal rejects the employer's purported reason for dismissal, it may conclude that this gives credence to the reason advanced by the employee, and it may find that the reason was the one asserted by the employee. However, it is not obliged to do so. The identification of the reason will depend on the findings of fact and inferences drawn from those facts."

Dahou is of particular relevance because it contains further comments on this point from the Court of Appeal. It should be noted that *Osipov* also went to the Court of Appeal but no comment was made about the EAT's observations on the burden of proof. The Court of Appeal in *Dahou* suggest that in trade union detriment cases the burden on the claimant is to raise only a prime facie case for causation (see paras. 26, 31 and 37 and compare to the more onerous wider burden suggested by *Osipov*) and gave a more encouraging reflection on the circumstances when an inference will be drawn (subsection (c) in *Osipov*, above), observing at para. 40:

> "As regards dismissal cases, this court has held (*[Kuzel v Roche Products Ltd* [2008] IRLR 530], paragraph 59) that an employer's failure to show what the reason for the dismissal was does not entail the conclusion that the reason was as asserted by the employee. As a proposition of logic, this applies no less to detriment cases. Simler J did not hold that it would never follow from a respondent's failure to show his reasons that the employee's case was right. Usually no doubt it will...."

Claimants may seek to argue that the more beneficial explanation of the burden of proof by the Court of Appeal in *Dahou* should be preferred to that of the EAT in *Osipov*. Conversely, respondents will answer that they concern two different protections and will note that Simler P in *Osipov* referred to the 'prime facie' approach to the burden of proof that exists for dismissal cases (see below) and made a conscious distinction to detriment cases. The resolution of any conflict will be an important point in how whistleblowing detriment cases are resolved.

Applying the burden of proof provisions, the question for a tribunal is whether the act or omission complained of was done "on the ground that" the worker made a protected disclosure and this test is notably different for a claim relating to dismissal under s.103A ERA 1996, as discussed below.

The relevant test is whether a protected disclosure "materially influences (in the sense of being more than a trivial influence) the employer's treatment of the whistleblower" *Fecitt v NHS Manchester* [2012] IRLR 64, para. 65). Fecitt should be treated with a note of caution for some other aspects of its reasoning because it was decided before the changes of the ERRA 2013 came into effect on 25 June 2013 and indeed, some of the changes made by that legislation respond to points highlighted in *Fecitt*.

In considering this aspect, a tribunal will take a similar approach to the discrimination test of considering "the reason why" and considering the personal motivation of the person that committed the alleged detriment (*Chief Constable of West Yorkshire Police v Khan* [2001] UKHL 48; Harrow London Borough v Knight [2003] IRLR 140; *Gibson v London Borough of Hounslow & Anor* [2018] (UKEAT 0033/18/2012, Unreported, December 2018) at para. 37). In *Khan* at para. 29, Lord Nicholls stated that the question to be asked is:

"why did the alleged discriminator act as he did? Unlike causation, this is a subjective test. Causation is a legal conclusion. The reason why a person acted as he did is a question of fact."

In applying this "subjective test", the Tribunal is therefore not required to carry out a value judgment or critique of the decisions made by the Respondent. This test requires the Tribunal simply to look at the motivation of the Respondent. A simple application of the 'but for' test is erroneous (*Knight*), as is a determination based solely on intent (*James v Eastleigh Borough Council* [1990] IRLR 288) or motive (*Grieg v Community Industry* [1979] IRLR 158).

It is also essential that a tribunal consider whether the act or omission was on the ground of the disclosure itself, or some other related feature (*Martin v Devonshires Solicitors* [2011] ICR 352). The Court of Appeal in *Beatt v Croydon Health Services NHS Trust* [2017] EWCA Civ 401 at para. 35 summarised this point, observing:

> "In *Panayiotou v Chief Constable of Hampshire Police* [2014] UKEAT/0436/13, [2014] IRLR 500, the EAT (Lewis J sitting alone) held that it was in principle possible to distinguish, for the purpose of section 47B, between the fact that a worker had made a protected disclosure and the manner in which they did so: if the detriment complained of occurred on the ground of the latter and not the former the employer will not be liable."

For a recent example where the *Panayiotou* distinction was found and a detriment claim therefore failed (upheld on appeal), see *Gibson v London Borough of Hounslow & Anor* [2018] (UKEAT 0033/18/2012, Unreported, December 2018), which relied upon the finding that it was the Claimant's "ungovernability" (para. 53) that was the cause of detriment. However, this distinction between the fact that the worker has made a protected disclosure and the manner in which they did so will not always be possible. In *Beatt* itself the Trust failed in its argument on the causation of dismissal to distinguish between the fact that a protected disclosure had been made as opposed to a belief that the dismissals were not made in good faith.

If a Claimant complains of their **dismissal**, regard must be had to s.47B(2) ERA 1996:

> "(2) This section does not apply where —
>
> (a) the worker is an employee, and

(b) the detriment in question amounts to dismissal (within the meaning of Part X)."

This subsection provides essentially that a complaint of dismissal itself should not be made as a detriment claim. Instead, s.103A ERA 1996 provides a complaint of unfair dismissal. This is a significant point because the threshold for establishing causation under s.103A is that "the principal reason" must be a protected disclosure, rather than the lower threshold of simply 'material influence', per *Fecitt*. The Court of Appeal's judgment in *Timis & Anor v Osipov & Anor* [2018] EWCA Civ 2321 of October 2018 is highly relevant to these considerations as it considers the extent to which a Claimant can claim not for unfair dismissal under s.103A but as a detriment claim under s.47B for "losses which flowed from the claimant's dismissal". This was relevant for the Claimant in *Osipov* because his previous employer had gone insolvent and he therefore sought to claim against his previous directors personally for their role in causing his dismissal. The detriment relied upon is quoted at para. 35 as "Any instructions or recommendations given by the 2nd to 5th Respondents which culminated in the Claimant's dismissal". The Court of Appeal's discussion of the point develops from paragraph 47 and comments include the relevance of tainted decisions, as discussed below regarding s.103A claims. In considering the application of s.47B(2), Underhill LJ emphasises the need to not "confuse the detriment of which the worker complains with the loss caused by that detriment", observing at para.81:

"the "detriment in question" in sub-section (2) must be the detriment to which the claimant complains that he or she has been subjected contrary to section 47B (1) or (1A) – in other words, his or her cause of action – which in a case of the kind which we are now considering is not the dismissal but the distinct prior act which caused it."

After a thorough analysis, the conclusion is clear at paras. 84 and 91:

> "section 47B (2) places no barrier to recovery of compensation for losses flowing from a dismissal which was itself caused by a prior act of whistleblower detriment. For the avoidance of doubt, such compensation would be subject to the usual rules about remoteness and discounting for contingencies (including the contingency that the employment might have terminated in any event)"

This is a tricky issue and Underhill LJ notes that "the tribunal's reasoning is obscure" (para. 42) and himself relies on analysis that he observes is "regrettably dense" (para. 91). *Osipov* is a highly significant case and may pave the way for some astute Claimants to claim losses caused by a detrimental action that caused dismissal rather than dismissal itself, whereas some Respondents may feel this is simply side-stepping the higher evidential threshold of s.103A ERA 1996.

Dismissal under s.103A ERA 1996

s.103A ERA 1996 provides:

> "An employee who is dismissed shall be regarded for the purposes of this Part as unfairly dismissed if the reason (or, if more than one, the principal reason) for the dismissal is that the employee made a protected disclosure."

Unlike a claim of 'ordinary' unfair dismissal, there is no qualifying period of service required to issue a claim under s.103A, per s.108(3)(ff) ERA 1996. If though an employee claiming under s.103A does have the required two years length of service for a claim of 'ordinary unfair dismissal', they are entitled to and often do issue such a claim alongside, pursuant to s.94 ERA 1996. Such a claim can only be made by an 'employee'; being a worker who does not have the status of employee is not enough. See the 'Who Can Be a Whistleblower' chapter for further discussion.

As highlighted above, the evidential threshold in a claim under s.103A is higher than in a claim of detriment under s.47B. See the contrast between "the principal reason" test and that of 'material influence'. Elias LJ in *Fecitt* accepted that "this creates an anomaly" but stated succinctly, "if Parliament had wanted the test for the standard of proof in section 47B to be the same as for unfair dismissal, it could have used precisely the same language, but it did not do so". The assessment of causation is a matter of fact for the tribunal to assess and any perceived unfairness to Claimants of this anomaly may to some extent be obviated by *Osipov* (Court of Appeal), discussed above.

The burden of proof provisions for a whistleblowing dismissal claim were summarised by Simler P in the EAT hearing of *Osipov*, cited as *International Petroleum Ltd & Ors v Osipov & Ors* [2017] UKEAT 0058/17/1907 at para. 116:

> "In a s.103A ERA 1996 case, the correct approach to the burden of proof was set out in *Kuzel v. Roche* at paragraphs 58-60 as follows:
>
> (a) the employee must produce some evidence to suggest that his dismissal was for the principal reason that he made protected disclosure.
>
> (b) The burden then shifts to the employer to show that the dismissal was for a potentially fair reason.

(c) If the employer fails to show the reason for the dismissal, then the employment tribunal may draw an inference (where such inference is appropriate) that the true reason for the dismissal was that suggested by the employee.

(d) However, at paragraph 60 of *Kuzel v. Roche* the CA held:

> "As it is a matter of fact, the identification of the reason or principal reason turns on direct evidence and permissible inferences from it. It may be open to the tribunal to find that, on a consideration of all the evidence in the particular case, the true reason for dismissal was not that advanced by either side. In brief, an employer may fail in its case of fair dismissal for an admissible reason, but that does not mean that the employer fails in disputing the case advanced by the employee on the basis of an automatically unfair dismissal on the basis of a different reason".

'Tainted decisions', i.e. when a decision is made not itself directly because of a prohibited reason but based on someone else's view that *was* influenced by a prohibited reason, have been an important topic in tribunals since Underhill LJ's judgment in *CLFIS (UK) Ltd v Reynolds* [2015] EWCA Civ 439. The facts of *Reynolds* are summarised by Underhill LJ's later judgment in *Osipov* (Court of Appeal):

> "The decision-maker had not been motivated by her age, but he had relied on a report from another employee who it was suggested might have been so motivated. It was relevant to consider whether, even though the claimant could not base any claim on the dismissal decision itself, she could rely on the prior act of the author of the report as a detriment which had caused her dismissal and on that basis recover against the

employer for the losses consequent on that dismissal. It was held that she could."

It will be noted that the principle from *Reynolds* is not that causation is therefore established for the decision to dismiss, rather that recovery can be achieved for the same losses that would be claimed if causation were so established by a claim based on an actions that led to the dismissal. *Reynolds* was a discrimination case but the principles were examined again by Underhill LJ in the context of a PIDA claim in *Royal Mail Group v Jhuti* [2017] EWCA Civ 1632, [2018] IRLR 251. The principles of *Reynolds* were stated in *Jhuti* at para. 32 to be:

"(1) Even if the motivation of the report-maker(s) was tainted that would not impugn the dismissal decision, because the only relevant question was what had motivated the decision-taker.

(2) However, that approach did not necessarily mean that in such a case a claimant could not recover compensation for the dismissal, since he or she could in principle rely on the making of the unfavourable report as an act of unlawful discrimination in its own right, for which the employer was liable. As I put it at para. 39 (5) (p. 1026 G-H):

"The losses caused to [the claimant] by her dismissal could be claimed for as part of the compensation for [that] discriminatory act, since they would have been caused or contributed to by that act and would not (at least normally) be too remote.""

The first principle of *Reynolds* was approved in relation to PIDA claims in *Jhuti* at paras. 64-65 and the second at para. 78. In *Osipov*, Underhill LJ noted that permission to appeal in *Jhuti* had been granted but nevertheless gave fresh affirmation to its conclusion, providing analysis at paras. 79-84 including "strong policy reasons" why that must be correct.

CHAPTER FIVE
REMEDY

This chapter will look at the important consideration of what remedies are available in a whistleblowing claim, focusing on the process within an employment tribunal. A tribunal's ability to award certain remedies are prescribed by legislation and commonly focus on the award of financial compensation.

It is best practice, if not essential, to consider at the outset of a claim or defence what may be the likely outcome. A claimant may want, for example, an apology or reference for future employment, but will find once they have issued a claim that this can only be achieved through negotiation and is not something that a tribunal can order. An employment tribunal is often referred to as 'a creature of statute' and as such, its powers and abilities to award compensation are set by legislation and are mostly restricted to financial compensation. Reflecting English law as a whole, a financial award made by a tribunal is designed to compensate the successful Claimant for identifiable loss, not punish the un-successful Respondent for their actions.

Interim Relief

Although rarely used in practice, it is prudent to consider a claim for interim relief first because if pursued, such a claim must be made first chronologically and within 7 days of the effective date of termination. Such a claim is made pursuant to s.128 ERA 1996 and the extremely short time limit is set out in subsection 2.

This remedy can only be claimed by employees and must be part of a claim that dismissal was because of a PID, as per s.103A ERA, rather than purely a detriment claim. A claim for interim relief can also be used for other types of claim outside of the whistleblowing context, principally those relating to automatically unfair reasons for dismissal (outlined at s.128(1) ERA). Although the 7-day time limit in s.128 ERA does not refer to the ACAS EC regime, because this remedy will be claimed as part of a claim relating to dismissal at s.103A ERA 1996, the ACAS EC regime will likely apply.

Part of the justification for the uniquely short time limit is the uniquely dramatic effect that a successful application for interim relief can have pursuant to s.129 ERA. The interim relief claimed is essentially to keep the employee's job alive, whether in practice or simply by the payment of salary to the employee. Set out in subsections 3 to 9, the tribunal shall:

(i) Ask the employer if they are willing to reinstate the employee or re-engage them on a comparable role;

(ii) If the employer and employee are willing for reinstatement or re-engagement, this shall be ordered.

(iii) If the employer refuses, the employee's pay and continuous employment status shall continue.

(iv) If the employee reasonably refuses an offer for reinstatement or re-engagement, the employee's pay and continuous employment status shall continue.

(v) If the employee's refusal is unreasonable, no order shall be made.

There is no automatic expectation that the employee will have to pay back any award, even if they lose the subsequent claim, although in theory it may be possible for an employer to achieve this in certain circumstances, such as material non-disclosure of an employee's new job, and is arguably a power expressly provided by the tribunal's ability to revoke or vary an order for interim relief before the determination or settlement of a claim, pursuant to s.131 ERA.

As this is a rarely seen application some readers may wonder why it is so uncommon, given how dramatic and beneficial for employees is an interim relief order. The reason and the expected catch is that as well as the short time limit, an order can only be made where a tribunal considers that it is "likely" that the claim under s.103A shall succeed.

Furthermore, "likely" denotes a high threshold and "does not simply mean more likely than not" (*Wollenberg v Global Gaming Ventures (Leeds) Limited & Ors.* (UKEAT/0053/18, Unreported, 4 April 2018), para. 25. In *Wollenberg* HHJ Richardson in the EAT explained the narrow test for successful interim relief application, stating at para.25:

> "it connotes a significant higher degree of likelihood. The Tribunal should ask itself whether the Applicant has established that he has a pretty good chance of succeeding in the final application to the Tribunal"

If pursued, the application should be determined by a tribunal "as soon as practicable after receiving the application" (s.128(3) ERA) and the employer shall be given not less than 7-days notice of the hearing together with a copy of the application (s.128(4) ERA). The Tribunal's usual powers of postponement are curtailed to only be used if "special circumstances exist". For an analysis of what constitutes special circumstances, see *Lunn v Aston Derby & Ors.*

(UKEAT/0039/18, Unreported, 26 February 2018), in which the EAT held that this did not mean "exceptional" and held that the availability of direct access Counsel did constitute special circumstances, in the context of difficulties in arranging alternative representation and a proposed delay of just 5 days.

The procedure for a hearing is outlined at *Wollenberg*, paras. 25 and 42:

> "a brief urgent hearing at which the Employment Judge must make a broad assessment... intended to be broad assessments by an Employment Judge who cannot be expected to grapple with vast quantities of material...no great reputational importance can be invested in the outcome of an interim hearing application. It is only a preliminary view taken by an Employment Judge in a case which will have to be in due course the subject the detailed investigation."

Reinstatement and re-engagement

Reinstatement (the Claimant gets their old job back) and re-engagement (the Claimant is engaged by the Respondent in an alternative post) are potential remedies to employees who have been dismissed, pursuant to ss.112-113 ERA. The principles that apply to these remedies for a Claimant unfairly dismissed as a result of a protected disclosure are the same as those applying to those unfairly dismissed under the general unfairness test of s.94 ERA and as such the detail applying to such orders can be found elsewhere but an overview is below. These remedies are only available to dismissed employees and not workers, as highlighted by Sir Robert Francis QC's Freedom to Speak Up report at 9.8, following recommendations to address this limitation at 7.3.

The Claimant has to 'express a wish' for either or both remedies. There is express inclusion for this within the ET1 form but failure to tick the right box will not prohibit a Claimant for later seeking such an order. The tribunal is required to explain the options to a Claimant and ask for their views, per s.112(2) ERA.

Reinstatement is summarised succinctly by s.114(1) ERA as, "an order that the employer shall treat the complainant in all respects as if he had not been dismissed". Contractual rights must be restored and any benefits that would have accrued but for dismissal must be applied as if dismissal had not occurred.

Re-engagement is defined at s.115(1) ERA and provides for wider possibilities than re-instatement. A tribunal can order engagement "by the employer, or by a successor of the employer or by an associated employer, in employment comparable to that from which he was dismissed or other suitable employment". This may be more relevant in the NHS than in other sectors because the individual employer, such as a Trust or Health Board, may operate across many different sites and therefore have increased opportunity to re-engage the dismissed employee at a place of work different to their original, therefore potentially avoiding the problems that led to the breakdown in the relationship and dismissal.

A tribunal's discretion whether to order reinstatement or re-engagement should be exercised in accordance with s.116 ERA. Broadly, this requires a consideration of the Claimant's "wishes", whether it is practicable for the proposed employer to comply and if the Claimant caused or contributed to their dismissal, whether it would be just to make such an order. There is extensive case law on these considerations but pertinent and modern cases include Central and North West London NHS Foundation Trust v Abimbola [2009] All ER (D) 188 (Aug) (confirming that a breakdown in mutual trust and confidence will mean it is not practicable to re-employ and exploring the relevance of a Claimant's dishonesty at a remedy hearing to this principle), Lincolnshire County Council v Lupton [2016] IRLR 576 (Simler P considering the extent of duty on a potential employer, specifically that there is no automatic requirement to dismiss an existing employee to facilitate the dismissed employee's re-engagement) and Dafiaghor-Olomu v Community Integrated Care and Cornerstone Community Care [2018] ICR 585 (Simler P allowing an appeal where the employer did not provide evidence of vacancies and the tribunal did not explore the employee's willingness to work outside her previous geographical area).

Compensation for unfair dismissal, financial loss and detriment remedies

The Court of Appeal in *Osipov* record that "Formally, reinstatement or re-engagement are the primary remedies, in the sense that the tribunal can only make an award of compensation where it has decided not to make an order under section 113 [ERA]". The Court of Appeal is of course correct but undoubtedly recognised that the most common form of remedy awarded by tribunals is financial compensation, whether in a claim of unfair dismissal or a detriment because of a protected disclosure.

If a whistleblower succeeds in a claim under s.103A ERA by demonstrating that the principal reason for their dismissal was a protected disclosure and it was therefore unfair, a tribunal will broadly follow the same principles of compensation as for a claim of 'ordinary' unfair dismissal and consider ordering a basic award, compensatory award and any other ancillary awards such as a week's wages, or other nominal sum, for loss of statutory rights. The basic award is prescribed by a statutory formula set out at s.119 ERA and potential reductions at s.122.

The compensatory award is designed to reflect financial loss and in practice will reflect lost earnings. Potential reductions are set out at s.123 ERA and general principles will apply such as a Claimant's duty to take reasonable steps to mitigate their loss (s.123(4) and *Wilding v British Telecommunications PLC* [2002] IRLR 524) and the potential for loss to have occurred in a hypothetical (*Polkey v AE Dayton Services Ltd* [1988] ICR 142 HL). For NHS staff, consideration should be given to any contractual nuances to ensure that in trying to recreate lost earnings an accurate hypothetical is constructed, such as any on-call supplements, loss or gain of private income due to the loss of NHS employment and how Programmed Activities would be arranged and Clinical Excellence Awards distributed in a Consultant's contract.

Significantly for an unfair dismissal arising because of a protected disclosure, the statutory cap outlined at s.124 ERA does not apply, as per s.124(1A). This is contrast to a claim of unfair dismissal pursuant to s.94 and there is therefore in theory no limit to the compensation that can be ordered for a successful claim under s.103A. An employer is however free to employ other arguments to limit compensation, as set out above in relation to s.123 ERA.

In a detriment claim, compensation can also be claimed for financial loss. As with financial loss arising from an unfair dismissal, this can include loss of salary as well as wider employment benefits and can in theory take into consideration related losses such as increased commute cost or business set up costs in an effort to mitigate loss. Evidence for all loss is of course essential. Financial loss arising from a protected disclosure detriment is prescribed by s.49 ERA and particular consideration should be given to sub-sections 1, 6 and 6A. s.49(6) states that if a worker suffers a detriment by the termination of their employment, the compensation payable cannot exceed that payable under s.103A.

In instances involving aggravating features of a relevant worker's right, consideration could be given to a request that a financial penalty is paid to the Secretary of State, in accordance with s.12A Employment Tribunals Act 1996.

Good faith

Common to the financial compensation awarded in respect of both protected disclosure dismissal and detriment claims is the potential for a reduction of up to 25% if the protected disclosure was not made in "good faith". The potential for a detriment claim is at s.49(6A) ERA, for a compensatory award in a dismissal claim at s.123(6A) and in both cases the tribunal may exercise its discretion "if it considers it just and equitable in all the circumstances".

These sections mark one of the changes enacted by the Enterprise and Regulatory Reform Act 2013 with effect from 25 June 2013. Prior to the ERRA, a disclosure would only count as a protected disclosure if made in good faith, whereas the ERRA moved the question of good faith to a consideration of how much compensation would be awarded. As succinctly stated by Underhill LJ in *Chesterton Global Ltd & Anor v Nurmohamed & Anor* (Rev 1) [2018] 1 All ER 947 after a useful summary of the changes, "the question of good faith is no longer relevant to liability in a whistleblowing case but it remains relevant to remedy".

Although the point at which good faith has changed, its meaning must surely have remained the same as pre-ERRA because the term is exactly the same. There is support for this view in *Saad v Southampton University Hospitals NHS Trust* [2018] IRLR 1007, in which the EAT considered the extent to which the good faith principles of whistleblowing law can be read across to the bad faith principles of victimisation under s.27 Equality Act 2010. The

Claimant was a Specialist Registrar and at tribunal was unsuccessful in a protected disclosure claim because it was held that his disclosure was not made in good faith. The tribunal then applied this finding to his victimisation claim, dismissing that also because they found that their finding in relation to the protected disclosure claim meant that his alleged Protected Act must have been made in bad faith. The EAT held that this was an error to simply apply the principles from one regime to another but in analysing the issue, the pre-ERRA consideration of good faith was applied and there was no suggestion that any other or new approach was required.

The meaning of good faith is explained by *Street v Derbyshire Unemployed Workers Centre* [2005] ICR 97. A disclosure is not made in good faith if the predominant purpose of making it was something other than "the declared public interest purpose of this legislation" (para. 56), such as out of personal antagonism. Further, at para. 73 a worker will not be making a disclosure in good faith if:

"his or her predominant motivation for disclosing information was not directed to remedying the wrongs identified in section 43B, but was an ulterior motive unrelated to the statutory objectives."

The antithesis between an ulterior motive and good faith was further affirmed in *Korashi v Abertawe Bro Morgannwg University Local Health Board* [2012] IRLR 4 EAT and the explanation from *Street* affirmed in *Beatt v Croydon Health Services NHS Trust* ([2017] EWCA Civ 401 at para.26.

Injury to Feelings

Commonplace in awards for discrimination, compensation for injury to feelings represents the legal system's best attempt at putting a value on the emotional upset caused by a prohibited act. An award for injury to feelings is not available in a claim of unfair dismissal, as confirmed by the House of Lords in *Dunnachie v Kingston-upon-Hull Council* [2005] 1 AC 226.

However, in a situation exposed as potentially inconsistent in claims including those relating to a protected disclosure, an award for injury to feelings is available for a detriment claim. This was analysed by the EAT in *Virgo Fidelis Senior School v Boyle* [2004] ICR 1210 and the decision was held on the basis that the "loss" a Claimant is entitled to in a detriment claim under s.49 ERA has a wider meaning than that in an award for unfair dismissal and does extend to injury to feelings.

There have been doubts expressed over this point of law, partly because of the inconsistency exposed. A claim for unfair dismissal that was because of a protected disclosure does not attract an award for injury to feelings, but a claim for a detriment that may be linked to the dismissal, including very directly as in *Osipov*, can attract such compensation. Further doubts have been explored because a very similar provision to that under s.49 ERA that provides for "any loss" in the Working Time Regulations 1998 was held by the Court of Appeal to not include an award for injury to feelings in *Gomes v Higher Level Care Ltd* [2018] IRLR 440. However, these arguments were noted by the later Court of Appeal decision in *Osipov* (see para. 27 and note 3), which recorded the arguments but as none of the parties invited the Court to decide the point, it was determined that – for now – the correct approach is to proceed on the basis that *Virgo Fidelis* was correctly decided and injury to feelings awards are therefore available if a Claimant has suffered as a result of detriment arising from a protected disclosure.

Virgo Fidelis also confirmed that the guidelines from *Vento v Chief Constable of West Yorkshire Police (No. 2)* [2003] IRLR 102 should apply to an assessment of quantum when assessing an award for injury to feelings in a protected disclosure detriment case (paras. 45-46). Furthermore, the EAT in *Virgo Fidelis* gave indication as to where on the guidelines an award should fall when stating, "detriment suffered by 'whistle-blowers' should normally be regarded by Tribunals as a very serious breach of discrimination legislation" (para.45). Practitioners will be familiar with the 3 *Vento* bands used as the starting point for assessment of injury to feelings awards in discrimination claims and for historic claims will need to consider the Presidential Guidance issued on 23 March 2018 and 5 September 2017 to ensure that assessment is made using the correct level of inflation and other adjustments for the date the claim was issued. Finally, the consideration outlined above regarding good faith will also apply to an award for injury to feelings because the award, as with financial loss, stems from the same definition of loss at s.49 ERA.

Each case will of course turn on its own facts and the loss suffered and evidence available in each case will have to be considered on an individual basis. The main heads of loss that may stem from a whistleblowing claim are outlined above but in appropriate cases, consideration will have to be given to further nuances, such as a claim for personal injury, aggravated damages and a reduction or increase for failure to follow an ACAS code.

CHAPTER SIX
CONTEMPORARY AND
FUTURE ISSUES

In this final section, topics of interest at present and anticipated in the future will be discussed. This book has focused on the practical application of NHS Whistleblowing and the Law, but this final chapter will explore some of the key current developments of this topic and discuss some anticipated issues. The increased scrutiny and coverage of NHS whistleblowing that resulted in and developed from the Freedom to Speak Up report will first be addressed, followed by a look at legislation, the relevance to non-disclosure agreements and finally a return to practicalities by discussing sources of advice and funding.

Freedom to Speak Up and Whistleblowing Guardians

In February 2015, a team led by Sir Robert Francis QC published Freedom to Speak Up, describing itself as "an independent review into creating an open and honest reporting culture in the NHS". It can be read in full at http://freedomtospeakup.org.uk. It was the result of consultation with healthcare professionals across England in a variety of fields and reports that this included a confidential online survey completed by 19,764 staff and 612 people writing to the review to share their experiences. The review emerged from what the executive summary describes as "continuing disquiet about the way NHS organisations deal with concerns raised by NHS staff and the treatment of some of those who have spoken up". This in part feeds into and is fed by a number of legal claims that have exposed ill-treatment of whistleblowers and other fields of public scrutiny such as the Mid-Staffordshire inquiries, reflected by only 72% of respondents to the 2013 NHS staff survey who reported as being confident that it was safe to raise a concern.

The report recognises the limitations of protection from the legislation existing at the time, describing the ERA 1996 as "the legislation which theoretically provides protection for whistleblowers...at best the legislation provides a series of remedies after detriment" (exec. summary paras. 11-12), but little substantial legislative changes have been implemented since the report's release.

The recommendations of the review are set out across 20 'Principles', such as Culture of Safety, Culture of Raising Concerns and Culture Free From Bullying, each with corresponding 'Actions' of practical steps that NHS organisations, staff, regulators and the executive should implement.

Whistleblowing Guardians: Principle 11, "Support", made a strong recommendation for all NHS organisations to appoint a person whose dedicated role is to oversee the raising of concerns by recognition of their independence and impartiality, universal access to speak with anyone in or outside the NHS organisation and "tenacity to ensure safety issues are addressed". Importantly, this role is a person to whom staff can go without fear with their concerns and by a universal job title, will be understood across organisations as the person performing this role. The term 'Guardian' has been adopted from the review for this role and by the NHS Contract (2016/17) all NHS trusts and foundation trusts are required to nominate a Freedom to Speak Up Guardian. Employees should know from their local policy what steps to take if they have a concern and at what point to involve their Guardian.

Advising NHS organisations and the local Guardians is the National Guardian, currently Dr Henrietta Hughes. The National Guardian's role is emphatically stated by its webpages (within the CQC website) that it is not a regulator, although it also confirms it is a Prescribed Person for the purposes of s.43F ERA 1996. Its role is to advise local Guardians on best practice to enable staff to speak up safely, and feel that they can do so, and again states that it will not intervene to investigate individual cases or supplant local processes. The National Guardian's role is intended to reflect Sir Robert Francis QC's Principle 15 'External Review, which warned against a further external body adding "delays and additional layers of bureaucracy" (exec. summary para. 74), but for some the limitations in the National Guardian's role is a missed opportunity to combine the powers of a regulator with a focus on whistleblowing. WhistleblowersUK, a not for profit organisation that seeks to support whistleblowers, calls for a national Office for the Whistleblower, whose powers would go far beyond those of the National Guardian and include monitoring and intervening in individual cases.

The idea that it is good practice to have a designated person to progress and deal with concerns raised has been recognised outside of the NHS in other regulated industries. In finance, for example, the Financial Conduct Authority issued a policy statement that required relevant firms to appoint a 'whistleblowers' champion' by September 2016 (see policy statement 15/24 and part SYSC 18 of the FCA Handbook).

Legislative Developments

The Freedom to Speak Up report concludes chapter 9, Extending Legal Protection, with a recognition that current legislative protection is "weak" (para. 9.17) but not advocating a wholesale review for various reasons, including that the report focused on the NHS, whereas legislative changes to PIDA 1998 and ERA 1996 may have inadvertent consequences for other sectors.

However, the report made an exception for one area, which it was stated needs strengthening because "individuals are suffering, or are at risk of suffering, serious detriments in seeking re-employment in the health service after making a protected disclosure" (para. 9.19). That recommendation resulted in the Employment Rights Act 1996 (NHS Recruitment – Protected Disclosure) Regulations 2018, discussed above.

Beyond those Regulations, there appears to be currently little prospect of dramatic changes to whistleblowing law any time soon, applicable to the NHS or outside. Alongside the 2018 NHS Recruitment Regulations, the government published very similar provision for Regulations to provide similar protection applicable to those working within children's social care. The power to enact Regulations for the children's social care sector is provided at s.32 Children and Social Work Act 2017, proposing an amendment to s.49C ERA 1996 that largely reflects the same power used to make the NHS 2018 Regulations at s.49B ERA. However, in contrast to the regulations in respect of NHS workers, no regulations in respect of children's social care have been enacted. Despite 5 different commencement regulations bringing into force other parts of the Children and Social Work Act 2017, the relevant part "prohibiting discrimination because of protected disclosure" and any subsequent regulations are not yet in force.

A topic gaining increasing publicity and support is the suggestion that whistleblowers should be paid as a reward for raising their concerns and as a form of compensation for the severe disruption that their protected disclosure can bring to their lives. It is argued that a financial incentive would encourage responsible whistleblowing and ensure that matters of public interest are raised and obviated before further damage is done. Currently, the UK has no such reward scheme and relies on the good intentions of individuals to raise their concerns. Although the tribunal system is aimed at providing compensation, even a whistleblower successful in their claim will commonly be left to pay for their own legal costs (as per the default rule) and may feel that the impact on their career and wider life leaves a lacuna in compensation. Such an incentive scheme would bring the UK in line with other jurisdictions, notably the US, where the Securities and Exchange Commission offer whistleblowers financial rewards of between 10-30% when a sanction of over $1 million is imposed based on information provided by the whistleblower. The SEC reports that it has awarded over £250 million to individuals since its first award in 2012, gained from over £1 billion in sanctions based on information provided by whistleblowers. The SEC states on its website, "by law, the SEC protects the confidentiality of whistleblowers and does not disclose information that might directly or indirectly reveal a whistleblower's identity" and further highlights that it is able to act on and reward information provided from abroad, including those in the UK who find themselves without such scheme in their own country.

Developments may come and significantly, as of July 2018 there is now an All-Party Parliamentary Group on Whistleblowing, but this is still in its infancy. There is a survey made by the APPG for whistleblowers to complete, with links on the websites of the APPG and Protect. Changes are most likely to be driven by the non-governmental organisations discussed below in relation to sources of advice.

The government itself has of course been preoccupied in recent years with Brexit and so the law in the field of whistleblowing in the UK, as in many other areas, has undergone little major development as Parliamentary time and attention is drawn elsewhere. At the time of writing, the reality of Brexit is still as unclear as many years ago and predictions about the legislative landscape if/after the UK/some part of the UK leaves the EU are speculative. Nevertheless, it would be surprising if the legislation currently in force that aims to protect whistleblowers is removed or dampened down after Brexit. Much of it did not originate in the EU and such dilution would be at odds with the contemporary focus on whistleblowing, as demonstrated by examples such as Freedom to Speak Up and the other issues explored in this chapter. It is assumed therefore that Brexit will not result in any significant changes in this area of law. The £350 million a week that the 'leave bus' suggested would be available to the NHS after Brexit could have much more impact, but 'unclear' and 'speculative' are perhaps the only appropriate and diplomatic terms for such expectations at the moment.

Moreover, a reduction in protection for whistleblowers, whether we leave the EU or not, would be at odds with a substantial and contemporaneous development of protection originating from the EU. April 2018 saw the European Commission release a 'Proposal for a Directive of the European Parliament and of the Council on the protection of persons reporting on breaches of Union law'. Since then, member states have debated the scope of the Directive, including whether the disclosure of tax matters should be excluded (reportedly opposed by Ireland, Luxembourg and Hungary) and the extent to which a person is required to make an internal disclosure before being protected. In March 2019, provisional agreement was reached by the European Parliament and member states for the proposed directive, including that disclosures relating to tax affairs and those made externally such as to a public authority will be protected. The proposed directive includes specified reporting procedures, including scope for when protection is provided when reporting to the media, obligations for employers and a prohibition on dismissal and other forms of detriment. In many ways, it thereby is similar to the regime under PIDA 1998 already implemented in the UK, although the detail of any key differences will emerge once the proposals develop formally. Before it becomes law, the new regime requires formal approval by the European Parliament and Council but the effect on the UK is unclear. To a degree, the protection adds relatively little to the existing UK legislation, certainly in contrast to other member states who lack comparative whistleblowing protection, but to the extent there are differences in protection, the ability of whistleblowers in the UK to rely on this new European protection is unclear until the realities of Brexit are clarified.

Non-Disclosure Agreements

Building on Principle 13 from Freedom to Speak Up, 'Transparency', and the warning against agreements that are simply void or at best "unnecessarily draconian", the use of non-disclosure agreements in settlement agreements has undergone close scrutiny within the NHS and far outside. Part of the momentum in this area has been gained from a focus on gender equality, notably by the '#metoo' movement and the exposure of various settlement agreements that sought to ensure the non-disclosure of various high-profile discrimination claims, both within the UK and abroad.

The ERA 1996 has always prohibited a contractual term that restricts whistleblowing, since PIDA 1998 was introduced and by the insertion of s.43J ERA:

"Contractual duties of confidentiality.

(1) Any provision in an agreement to which this section applies is void in so far as it purports to preclude the worker from making a protected disclosure.

(2) This section applies to any agreement between a worker and his employer (whether a worker's contract or not), including an agreement to refrain from instituting or continuing any proceedings under this Act or any proceedings for breach of contract."

Many commentators point out that even if s.43J is not technically breached, if a confidentiality clause appears too restrictive and if consequences of its breach are left too wide, the effect can be to nevertheless make the individual signatory feel that they have been gagged and fear making any disclosures that should otherwise be protected by s.43J. Sir Robert Francis QC's review observes in the executive summary (para.69):

> "Any confidentiality clauses which prevent a signatory from making a protected disclosure are void. I did not see any recent agreements which breached this. There were some however which contained restrictions that seemed unnecessarily draconian, and I can appreciate how individuals might think they were 'gagged'. This is a hindrance to transparency. Greater care needs to be taken in the drafting of confidentiality clauses, which should only be included if they are genuinely in the public interest. All settlement agreements should be available for inspection by the CQC."

These concerns about non-disclosure agreements have been repeated by other organisations, notably by the Equality and Human Rights Commission and Women and Equalities Committee, both of whom have turned their attention to lawyers, who it is suggested can sometimes be part of the problem in drafting over-restrictive and oppressive non-disclosure agreements on behalf of their clients. Such statements must be of interest to practitioners, not least because the Solicitors Regulation Authority and Law Society have issued formal guidance on these principles, advising members of appropriate practice. The SRA issued a warning notice in March 2018 and the Law Society issued a practice note in January 2019. The 2018 warning notice, which can be used by the SRA when exercising its regulatory functions, echoes the concerns expressed elsewhere and begins:

"...this warning notice, and the Handbook, should not be taken to prohibit the use of NDAs. However, we are concerned to ensure that you do not:

i.   use NDAs in circumstances in which the subject of the NDA may, as a result of the use of the NDA feel unable to notify the SRA or other regulators or law enforcement agencies of conduct which might otherwise be reportable

ii. use NDAs as a means of improperly threatening litigation or other adverse consequences, or otherwise exerting inappropriate influence over people not to make disclosures which are protected by statute, or reportable to regulators or law enforcement agencies."

Sources of Advice

It is assumed that NHS organisations will have in place tried and tested sources of advice and therefore this section is aimed primarily at individuals who may otherwise be lost in this complex area of law. Organisations without a source of advice would be well advised to consult their insurance policies to see if legal expenses insurance (LEI) is provided and some of the organisations below may also be able to assist in providing advice. Notably, Protect launched its 360 Benchmark in October 2018, aimed at helping organisations achieve best practice by "identifying gaps and providing organisations with an action plan on how to improve".

For individuals, in addition to trade unions and membership organisations such as the BMA and RCN, the following organisations may prove useful:

- Speak Up (https://speakup.direct/) is a service delivered on behalf of the Department for Health. It is aimed at those working within the NHS and social care sector and designed to provide advice and signposting about whitleblowing ('speaking up'). It provides a freephone number and online enquiry form.

- Protect (https://protect-advice.org.uk, formerly Public Concern at Work) is a whistleblowing charity that provides free, confidential advice to those concerned about malpractice or wrongdoing at work, as well as consultancy services to organisations to help with their whistleblowing arrangements. Their website and phoneline (020 3117 2520) provide extensive advice.

- WhistleblowersUK (https://www.wbuk.org/) is a not for profit company that is relatively new and focuses its work on whistleblowers rather than organisations. It provides advice, including about litigation and connecting with lawyers, and currently is campaigning for a national Office for the Whistleblower.

- FRU (http://www.thefru.org.uk/) provide employment law advice and representation for those with cases in the South East (principally London) or Nottingham. Their services are free and can be accessed after registration via a referral agency.

- Law Centres and Citizens Advice Bureaus. The former are more likely to have individuals with more legal experience but these two general sources of advice may be a useful source of free information or signposting.

Funding

Individuals seeking advice or representation without LEI or some over cover may be put off from engaging lawyers by the perceived cost. Reflecting today's connected world and the increased focus and awareness of NHS safety concerns and whistleblowing in general that can expose such issues, some individuals have been able to successfully crowdfund towards their legal costs. Sites including crowdjustice.com have enabled some to obtain representation and ensure a more equal footing in litigation.

MORE BOOKS BY
LAW BRIEF PUBLISHING

A selection of our other titles available now:-

'A Practical Guide to the SRA Principles, Individual and Law Firm Codes of Conduct 2019 – What Every Law Firm Needs to Know' by Paul Bennett
'A Practical Guide to Industrial Disease Claims' by Andrew Mckie & Ian Skeate
'Employment Law and the Gig Economy' by Nigel Mackay & Annie Powell
'A Practical Guide to Redundancy' by Philip Hyland
'A Practical Guide to Vicarious Liability' by Mariel Irvine
'A Practical Guide to Relief from Sanctions Post-Mitchell and Denton' by Peter Causton
'A Practical Guide to Immigration Law and Tier 1 Entrepreneur Applications' by Sarah Pinder
'Commercial Mediation – A Practical Guide' by Nick Carr
'A Practical Guide to Solicitor and Client Costs' by Robin Dunne
'Artificial Intelligence – The Practical Legal Issues' by John Buyers
'A Practical Guide to Marketing for Lawyers – 2nd Edition' by Catherine Bailey & Jennet Ingram
'A Practical Guide to Advising Schools on Employment Law' by Jonathan Holden
'A Practical Guide to the General Data Protection Regulation (GDPR)' by Keith Markham
'A Practical Guide to Digital and Social Media Law for Lawyers' by Sherree Westell
'Practical Mediation: A Guide for Mediators, Advocates, Advisers, Lawyers, and Students in Civil, Commercial, Business, Property, Workplace, and Employment Cases' by Jonathan Dingle with John Sephton
'On Experts: CPR35 for Lawyers and Experts' by David Boyle
'Employers' Liability Claims: A Practical Guide Post-Jackson' by Andrew Mckie

'The No Nonsense Solicitors' Practice: A Guide To Running Your Firm' by Bettina Brueggemann
'Baby Steps: A Guide to Maternity Leave and Maternity Pay' by Leah Waller
'The Queen's Counsel Lawyer's Omnibus: 20 Years of Cartoons from The Times 1993-2013' by Alex Steuart Williams

These books and more are available to order online direct from the publisher at www.lawbriefpublishing.com, where you can also read free sample chapters. For any queries, contact us on 0844 587 2383 or mail@lawbriefpublishing.com.

Our books are also usually in stock at www.amazon.co.uk with free next day delivery for Prime members, and at good legal bookshops such as Wildy & Sons.

We are regularly launching new books in our series of practical day-to-day practitioners' guides. Visit our website and join our free newsletter to be kept informed and to receive special offers, free chapters, etc.

You can also follow us on Twitter at www.twitter.com/lawbriefpub.

Printed in Great Britain
by Amazon

38041822R00059